Snuff Garrett
Record Producer

*Hal's seven Records of the Year
illustrate his consistency in the studio.
He was always right there, the anchor
of the session, as well as a great
player. He had the ability to turn the
emotional tide in a session, on these
dates when the other musicians were
ground down from fatigue, back to a
productive recording date thanks to
his quick wit and fast thinking.*
–Jimmy Webb
Songwriter/recording artist

*Hal Blaine set the standard for drum
sounds in the sixties. His unique style and
feeling provided the "motor" for some of
the most exciting recordings, including
"Taste of Honey" by Herb Alpert and the
Tijuana Brass.*
–Herb Alpert
Recording artist/
record company owner

*Hal Blaine could keep a horde
of politicians from dragging!*
–Jimmy Brown
Record Producer

About the cover:
Hal Blaine painting by Evan Johnson
concept by Mr. Bonzai
layout by Rob Cook

Hare Brain (as our Far East friends called Hal) is not only one of the most talented people I've ever worked with- he is by far the funniest.
–John Denver
Recording Artist

Hal Blaine marches to a different drummer– himself. And those of us who have had the pleasure to march along with him are richer for the good times he brings to music and life.
–Mason Williams
Recording Artist

I remember Hal as being the catalyst for making something happen musically on all of the record dates we worked. Hal's humor made many recording sessions that were very dull and non-musical somehow come alive and start happening.
–Don Randi
Studio Keyboardist

Hal is the most fantastic, creative and inventive studio drummer the music business has ever had.
–Carol Kaye
Studio bassist

Thanks, Hal, for the tom tom tom tom toms!
–Ringo Starr
Drummer

Hal Blaine was the most creative and helpful musician I've known in all my years in the recording business. I don't care if the singer was Elvis Presley or Little Bernie from Idaho, Hal Blaine's creative juices poured out the same. There will never be another drummer like Hal Blaine. The mold has been put to rest.
>   –Tom Tedesco
>   Studio guitarist

For a man who has seen it all in the West Coast pop music scene, it has certainly taken my friend Hal Blaine a long time to put it down on paper. It's done and I heartily recommend Hal Blaine and The Wrecking Crew to you.   –Henry Mancini
>   Composer/arranger

Hal Blaine is an original. Not only is he a great drummer, but a great person as well. Besides his talent on popular recordings, his attitude and sense of humor have livened and touched them all. I'm proud to say that Hal's playing has made the difference on many of my own records.
>   –Neil Diamond
>   Recording Artist

*If music in the second half
of the 20th century were
the Empire State Building,
Hal Blaine would be the
ground floor.*

> –Art Garfunkel
> Recording artist

*Our group had never sung with
anything but one acoustic guitar
until that fateful day in 1965
when we came together in
Studio 3 at Western Recorders.
There, The Mamas and the Papas
'sound' was created with the
distinctive beat that Hal Blaine
had already made himself
famous for.*

> –Michelle Phillips
> The Mamas & the Papas

*Hal had everything... he had
sound, feel and he had style – in
perfect proportion. He had great
ideas and execution and what
seemed to be the confidence to
say to everyone around him,
'This is right' – whether he was
saying it verbally of through
his playing. There are no more
Hal Blaines.*

> –Max Weinberg
> Drummer, E Street Band

HAL BLAINE
and The Wrecking Crew

Hal Blaine with Mr. Bonzai

edited by David M. Schwartz

Rebeats Publications
219 Prospect
Alma, Michigan 48801
www.rebeats.com

Hal Blaine And The Wrecking Crew
Third Edition

International Standard Book Number 978-1-888408-12-6

First published by Mixbooks, a division of Act III Publishing,
as ISBN #0-918371-01-5
edited by David M. Schwartz, co-founder, *Mix* Magazine
First Printing   1990
Second Printing   1993

First Rebeats edition published as ISBN #1-888408-07-3, 2003

Thanks to: Russ Wapensky of the U.S. State Department, Gary Gam,
Paul David Schaffer, Martha Lorini, Joe Kerger, Sally Ehrens, Frank
Interdonato, The Music Den, and Bill Peterson of Local 47.

Contents

Foreword by Jim Keltner
Introduction, 2009   Mr. Bonzai
Acknowledgments
Discography: Performances on Top Ten Records

Forward

The first time I heard Hal Blaine play was during a session at Sunset Sound in the early sixties. Although I wasn't supposed to be in the control room, I was magnetized by what I was hearing, and I had to see this incredible drummer.

I can hardly describe the effect he had on me. His command behind the drums was so strong and his sound was so good. He was playing a beat I'd heard thousands of times but was giving it a certain kind of sophisticated funk that I'd never heard before. His approach to studio drumming burned into my memory, and at the same time he became an awesome mystery to me as an up-and-coming drummer. How was he able to do these incredible things with his drums?

In 1965, when I joined Gary Lewis and the Playboys, I was just starting to play rock and roll. I was told that Hal Blaine was the man who played on all of the big rock and roll records, like Gary's first hit, *This Diamond Ring*. When we cut Gary's single *Just My Style,* Leon Russell, who co-wrote and arranged the song, guided me through the entire session. But when we began work on the album, there were a couple of songs that had me stumped for what to play. Hal came down to play tambourine one night, though I really think they brought him in because they weren't sure if I could handle everything.

The first thing that impressed me was that Hal was extremely nice and put me at ease. He didn't make me feel inferior or insecure, and that meant a lot to me. I also felt that I could ask him anything without feeling like a dodo. From that moment on, I would call Hal on the phone or track him down in the studio to explain things or show me how to play a tough part.

Rock and roll was just beginning to grow up when Hal arrived on the scene with all of his big band, jazz, and show drumming, and later added a whole new bag of tricks. He had the first monster drum kit with all of the extra tom-toms – not to impress anyone with quantity, but to stretch the range of the instrument with the variety of sounds and tones he heard in his head.

Hal was always able to find the groove, do exactly the right thing, but also make the presence of the drummer known and respected. His command and authority were different from the rest, and his personality played a big part in the success of so many of his sessions. When a session was falling apart, he would take command and put it back together again. He had an authoritative presence, and when he hit the drums you knew that he meant business.

As the art and science of recording grew up in the Sixties, and the drums played an increasing role in the sound of popular music, Hal sat at the center of the action.

Jim Keltner
Studio/Stage Drummer

Introduction (2010 edition)

As interest in Hal Blaine continues to grow and grow, we are pleased to present this third edition of his life story. Now in his Eighties, Hal explains that he is "semi-retired" and enjoying his home near Palm Springs. "The Wrecking Crew film directed by Denny Tedesco has created quite a stir and I've been doing a lot of interviews," Hal explains. "I've joined Denny and fellow musicians like Don Randi and producer Bones Howe for discussions after the film screenings and it's really a kick to talk with the younger generations of musicians and fans. It's a great film and really captures what we accomplished as session players on so many hits."

Hal tells me that he still enjoys a gig now and then, and recently collaborated with Don Randi playing instrumentals of Beach Boys and Mamas and Papas tunes for a skateboarding movie. He's also proud to still endorse Zildjian cymbals and his signature drumsticks, as well as Remo, which presented him on his 80th birthday with a drumhead autographed by great drummers from around the world. His daughter Michelle and her family have moved to Hawaii and got help settling in by Hal's dear friend Patti Smart, a former stewardess whom he used to date when he was playing the Islands with Tommy Sands in the Fifties. They are urging him to join them on Maui, but Hal seems to be enjoying himself just fine in the warm California desert, just a few hours away from the Hollywood studios where he has worked for so many years.

As you relive Hal's life story, why not put on a few tunes to get in the mood? Step into the studio with Hal and do some *California Dreamin'*, 1966. Get close to Dean Martin with *Everybody Loves Somebody*, 1964. Take off with The Byrds' *Mr. Tambourine Man*, 1965. Pick your favorite hit from the the Sixties into the Eighties and there's a good chance that Blaine was at the drums. *He's A Rebel*, 1962. *A Taste of Honey*, 1965. *Strangers In The Night*, 1966. *Mrs. Robinson*, 1968. *Song Sung Blue*, 1972. *Love Will Keep Us Together*, 1975. *Surfin USA*, 1963. *These Boots Are Made For Walkin*, 1966. *Aquarius/Let The Sun Shine*, 1969. *The Way We Were*, 1974. *Jose Cuervo*, 1981. The list of hits goes on and on, defining the sounds of a generation, and still conveying that era in films and television shows.

In the recording studios, the band drummers were relieved to have Blaine lock the song down, on time and to the quick approval of everyone involved – from the top man at the record company to the producer who had a "sound" in mind. It was a unique time in the history of music recording, and one we may never see again. Blaine was so busy, he invented "personalized" cartage so his monster kits could be set up correctly across town at the top studios.

Hal is now semi-retired, but still has a few kits in top shape. "I haven't been taking many gigs," he told me again this year. Hal picks and chooses what he wants to work on these days, is open to new and exciting projects, and concentrates on recording and performing with old friends and fellow members of the Crew.

The consummate session and stage joker, Hal actually recorded a CD of jokes in 1998, called "Buh-Doom!" Talk about rhythm and timing – his drum solos and hilarious stories reveal an important side of Hal's character, the humorist who often kept an uptight session from getting stalled.

To really appreciate Hal Blaine, you have to listen to a lot of music. This man was playing as many as eight dates a day! When all the drums were real. No drum machines, no sampling. So, with Hal, it's all real. Hal has sold most of his drum kits – one of them is at the Hard Rock Cafe in Seattle and another kit is in the NAMM Museum in Carlsbad, California. He is really proud of these hand-tooled gems that he designed, a percussive leap that would alter the sound of pop music. Ringo wanted a set, Karen Carpenter had to have a set, and countless others keep that big sound alive today.

"Normally, drummers were playing on a 4-piece set, sometimes, 5," he recalls. "My set was a 12-piece set with an octave of drums, so that I could do those long fills that you hear on songs by The Carpenters. Another early hit was Cher's *Half Breed*. The very first session I used them on was for an Al Wilson record called *The Snake*. And then, of course, everybody wanted them. I introduced that set on the Ed Sullivan Show. I did a solo with Nancy Sinatra singing *Drummer Man*. Absolutely changed the drum world. I was a Ludwig drummer, and we used all Ludwig hardware on the set, and they brought it out and called it "The Octoplus." Within months, every drum company was putting out a similar design."

Hal became the first sideman to be inducted into the Rock and Roll Hall of Fame, a category finally realized in 2000, after much lobbying by top artists who understood this often overlooked contribution to recorded hit music. He was honored, along with drummer pal Earl Palmer and Scotty Moore, Elvis' guitarist. Hal adds, with a chuckle, "I was the first Hall of Fame sideman because my name begins with B." In this book, you'll learn about Hal and his fellow musicians, known as "The Wrecking Crew" because they threw out their neckties, wore jeans and T-shirts, and turned the scene upside down. Together, they rose from the ranks of the serious studio cats the ones, as Hal often says, "who could read and play fly shit off the chart if it happened to be there." But times were changing, and the Crew also brought a new individualism to the meaning of "sideman."

The beauty of Hal's talent is that you can pick any one of the records that he played on and be transported to the moment – when there was no room for nothin' but the best.

Mr. Bonzai, Hollywood, November, 2009

Acknowledgements

I would like to dedicate this book to everyone with whom I have crossed paths during my long career, to those who have shared the ups and downs. I'd especially like to thank the great musicians for all their guidance while I was growing up, and the producers who gave me the opportunities to experiment and fulfill my dreams.

A special thanks to my daughter Michelle and my son David, who stuck it out through the death of their adoptive mother and the tough times of a musician's life.

Thanks to my sister Marcia and her wonderful family, who all had plenty of encouragement for me when things looked pretty bleak... to my brother Ben and his family, who had a place for me to flop and a sandwich while I was on the road and on the skids... to Mom and Dad, who lived long enough to see me on the Perry Como show and realized that maybe my musical ambitions were more than just a hobby... and to my sister Belle, who never saw my dream come true, but believed in me from the very beginning...

For my studio pals in The Wrecking Crew, I have only admiration and outrageous memories, which come back to me every time I turn on the radio. We created something that survives, an era of music that has a life of its own.

My thanks, of course, to all of the engineers and studio personnel who got me down on tape, and to all the artists, arrangers, and composers who befriended the kid from Holyoke and believed in what I was trying to say with my drums.

Finally I owe a special thanks to all of the drummers, past and present, who helped me shape my style while listening, watching, and emulating them. I couldn't a' done it without ya.

I hope that when you read these stories you will find inspration, that you take heart in your own abilities and shoot for your own dreams. Remember, there are no losers – only winners who give up too soon.

Discography:
Performances on Top Ten Records

CHART POSITION	SONG TITLE	ARTIST
1959		
10	*Baby Talk*	Jan and Dean
1960		
8	*Mama*	Connie Francis
1961		
1	*Can't Help Falling In Love With You*	Elvis Presley
4	*Where The Boys Are*	Connie Francis
1962		
1	*He's A Rebel*	The Crystals
2	*Return To Sender*	Elvis Presley
6	*The Lonely Bull*	Herb Alpert & TJB
1963		
6	*And Then He Kissed Me*	The Crystals
10	*Another Saturday Night*	Sam Cooke
2	*Be My Baby*	The Ronettes
6	*Be True to Your School/ /In My Room*	The Beach Boys
3	*Da Doo Ron Ron*	The Crystals
10	*Drag City*	Jan and Dean
10	*Eighteen Yellow Roses*	Bobby Darin
3	*She's A Fool*	Leslie Gore
5	*Surf City*	Jan and Dean
1	*Surfer Girl/Deuce Coupe*	The Beach Boys
7	*Surfin' USA*	The Beach Boys
3	*The Night Has 1000 Eyes*	Bobby Vee

3	*You're The Devil in Disguise*	Elvis Presley
3	*Zip a Dee Doo Dah*	Bobby Sox & Blue Jeans

1964

3	*Come A Little Bit Closer*	Jay & The Americans
8	*Dance Dance Dance*	The Beach Boys
8	*Dead Man's Curve*	Jan and Dean
5	*Fun Fun Fun*	The Beach Boys
1	*Everybody Loves Somebody*	Dean Martin
4	*Hey Little Cobra*	The Ripchords
1	*I Get Around*	The Beach Boys
9	*It's Over*	Roy Orbison
9	*Little Honda*	The Hondells
3	*Little Old Lady From Pasadena*	Jan and Dean
9	*Mountain of Love*	Johnny Rivers
3	*Out of Limits*	The Markettes
1	*Ringo*	Lorne Greene
6	*The Door Is Still Open*	Dean Martin

1965

*7	*A Taste of Honey*	Herb Alperb & TJB
3	*California Girls*	The Beach Boys
4	*Cara Mia*	Jay & The Americans
2	*Count Me In*	Gary Lewis & The Playboys
1	*Eve of Destruction*	Barry McGuire
4	*Everybody Loves A Clown*	Gary Lewis & The Playboys
1	*Help Me Rhonda*	The Beach Boys
8	*Hold Me, Thrill Me, Kiss Me*	Mel Carter
1	*I Got You Babe*	Sonny & Cher
1	*Mr. Tambourine Man*	The Byrds
10	*Red Roses For A Blue Lady*	Vic Dana
2	*Save Your Heart For Me*	Gary Lewis & The Playboys
7	*Seventh Son of a Seventh Son*	Johnny Rivers
1	*This Diamond Ring*	Gary Lewis & The Playboys
4	*You're The One*	The Vogues

1966

7	*Along Comes Mary*	The Association
2	*Barbara Ann*	The Beach Boys
4	*California Dreamin'*	The Mamas & The Papas
5	*Elusive Butterfly*	Bob Lind

1	*Good Vibrations*	The Beach Boys
9	*Guantanamera*	The Sandpipers
5	*Homeward Bound*	Simon & Garfunkel
7	*How's That Grab You Darlin'?*	Nancy Sinatra
3	*I Am A Rock*	Simon & Garfunkel
9	*I Couldn't Live Without Your Love*	Petula Clark
5	*I Saw Her Again Last Night*	
		The Mamas & The Papas
8	*If I were A Carpenter*	Bobby Darin
1	*Monday Monday*	The Mamas & The Papas
1	*My Love*	Petula Clark
3	*No Matter What Shape...*	The T-Bones
1	*Poor Side of Town*	Johnny Rivers
3	*She's Just My Style*	Gary Lewis & Playboys
9	*Sure Gonna Miss Her*	Gary Lewis & Playboys
3	*Sloop John B*	The Beach Boys
1	*Strangers In The Night*	Frank Sinatra
5	*Sugar Town*	Nancy Sinatra
4	*That's Life*	Frank Sinatra
1	*These Boots Were Made For Walkin'*	Nancy Sinatra
8	*Wouldn't It Be Nice*	The Beach Boys

1967

2	*A Little Bit Me*	The Monkees
3	*Baby I Need Your Lovin*	Johnny Rivers
3	*Come Back When You Grow Up*	Bobby Vee
5	*Creeque Alley*	The Mamas & The Papas
2	*Dedicated To The One I Love*	
		The Mamas & The Papas
5	*Him Or Me, What's It Gonna Be*	
		Paul Revere & The Raiders
8	*Let's Live For Today*	The Grass Roots
3	*Love, This Is My Song*	Petula Clark
2	*Never My Love*	The Association
4	*San Francisco, Wear Flowers*	Scott McKenzie
1	*Something Stupid*	Frank & Nancy Sinatra
1	*The Happening*	The Supremes
10	*Tracks Of My Tears*	Johnny Rivers
*7	*Up, Up and Away*	The Fifth Dimension
1	*Windy*	The Association

5	*Words of Love*	The Mamas & The Papas

1968

10	*Everything That Touches You*	The Association
5	*I Just Dropped In...*	First Edition
2	*MacArthur Park*	Richard Harris
5	*Midnight Confessions*	The Grass Roots
+*1	*Mrs. Robinson*	Simon and Garfunkel
7	*My Special Angel*	The Vogues
3	*Stoned Soul Picnic*	The Firth Dimension
7	*Turn Around, Look At Me*	The Vogues
2	*Young Girl*	Gary Puckett/Union Gap

1969

*1	*Aquarias/Let the Sun Shine*	The Firth Dimension
1	*Dizzy*	Tommy Roe
6	*Holly Holy*	Neil Diamond
4	*Galveston*	Glen Campbell
8	*Jam Up and Jelly Tight*	Tommy Roe
1	*Love Theme- Romeo and Juliet*	Henry Mancini
9	*This Girl's a Woman Now*	Gary Puckett/Union Gap
1	*Wedding Bell Blues*	The Fifth Dimension

1970

#*1	*Bridge Over Troubled Waters*	Simon and Garfunkel
4	*Cecelia*	Simon and Garfunkel
1	*Close to You*	The Carpenters
1	*Cracklin' Rosie*	Neil Diamond
2	*One Less Bell To Answer*	The Fifth Dimension
2	*We've Only Just Begun*	The Carpenters

1971

*1	*Cherish*	David Cassidy
6	*Doesn't Somebody Want To Be...*	The Partridge Family
4	*Don't Pull Your Love Out*	Hamilton, Joe Frank, & Reynolds
3	*For All We Know*	The Carpenters
4	*I Am, I Said*	Neil Diamond
1	*I Think I Love You*	The Partridge Family
9	*I'll Meet You Halfway*	The Partridge Family

1	*Indian Reservation*	Paul Revere & The Raiders
2	*Rainy Days & Mondays*	The Carpenters
9	*Sooner Or Later*	The Grass Roots
6	*Stoney End*	Barbara Streisand
2	*Superstar*	The Carpenters
9	*Theme From Love Story*	Andy Williams

1972

4	*Daddy Don't You Walk So Fast*	Wayne Newton
7	*Goodbye To Love*	The Carpenters
2	*Hurting Each Other*	The Carpenters
9	*I Need You*	America
5	*It Never Rains In Southern California*	
		Albert Hammond
8	*Last Night I Didn't Get To Sleep*	
		The Fifth Dimension
4	*Mother And Child Reunion*	Paul Simon
1	*Song Sung Blue*	Neil Diamond
8	*Ventura Highway*	America

1973

9	*All I Know*	Art Garfunkel
1	*Half Breed*	Cher
3	*Leave Me Alone*	Helen Reddy
2	*Yesterday Once More*	The Carpenters

1974

1	*Annie's Song*	John Denver
5	*Back Home Again*	John Denver
1	*The Way We Were*	Barbara Streisand
1	*Top of the World*	The Carpenters

1975

1	*I'm Sorry/Calypso*	John Denver
1	*Lizzy and the Rain Man*	Tanya Tucker
*1	*Love Will Keep Us Together*	The Captain and Tenille
1	*Thank God I'm A Country Boy*	John Denver

1976

1	*Theme From Mahogany*	Diana Ross
4	*Muskrat Love*	The Captain and Tenille

1978

    10   *You've Never Done It Like That*

                              The Captain and Tenille

1981

    1   *You're The Reason God Made Oklahoma*

                              Frizzell and West

    1   *Jose Cuervo*   Shelly West

    9   Texas State of Mind   Frizzell and West

* Grammy Record of The Year
+ Academy Award Song Of The Year
 # Album of the Year

HAL BLAINE
and The Wrecking Crew

1

The Holyoke Story

Harold Simon Belsky was born about 1 a.m., February 5. The year was 1929, the year of the crash. Rose and Meyer Isaac Belsky were immigrants. She came from Lithuania, he from Poland. They were Russian Jews who had been severely persecuted by the anti-Semites of the day and were fortunate, as 14-year-olds, to have been given visas to come to the "Promised Land," America.

My mom escaped death twice while growing up. She started working at a flour mill at about 3 years of age. She was working at the mill grinding flour with her mother and other townspeople when the Cossacks burst into the mill and started slaughtering the workers, mostly Lithuanian and Russian Jews. It was one of the early holocausts in Lithuania when the Russians were taking over the smaller countries now behind the Iron Curtain.

Another time, a Cossack soldier rode his horse down on her, sword held high, and was about to decapitate her when another soldier overtook him, picked up my mother, and rode to the nearby woods and threw her into the forest. She was about 7 at the time.

Mom and the other survivors hid for a very long time in the woods and the other underground hiding places that were soon established to save the children. For seven years they lived like rats with barely enough food to go around. Eventually the Lithuanian government, under the Russian czars, deported these unwanted Jews. Mom found herself on a cattle boat heading for Ellis Island, New York.

The crossing is a familiar story today. The struggle of the immigrants of those days, the filthy conditions of the crossing, the sickness and the sadness of the deaths of people within sight of shore. Yet these people died knowing that they were finally out from under the rule of the butchers and that their loved ones would soon walk free. .

At 13, my dad was a fisherman's helper on the Rhine River in Germany. His father had escaped the slaughters of Warsaw and had smuggled the family into Germany. He soon died and left the family to forage for themselves. In 1905 Dad was lucky enough to get onto a cattle boat and come to the US.

Both my parents were sent to Holyoke, Massachusetts, where they had cousins living. Holyoke was like a small Polish capital, loaded with immigrant Poles and jews from all over Europe. They all spoke Yiddish and worked from sunup to sundown. just a few years after my parents arrived, they met, fell in love and soon married and started raising a family. My sister Belle was the first born, followed by Marcia and my brother Ben, supposedly the last child.

Dad attended a tailor college and received a diploma. He started a small business with his two brothers, Ben and Jake, but they soon parted ways. He then took a job as a shoe repairman, continuing to work long hours. Dad was a very short man and a little hunchbacked; I can remember him moving crates and large boxes and never asking for help. He was a proud man and worked extremely hard.

Dad was earning $5 a week and feeding a family of five when I unexpectedly came into the world. It was a shock and a blow to the family. It was not the best of times to be born. They were barely existing on Dad's earnings as it was and the kids were too small to work. The market was about to crash and the US. was upside down. I probably should have been aborted but my parents were frightened of that sort of thing. (My dad's sister died on the table of a home abortionist years before I ever came along.)

We lived in Holyoke until I was 7 years old, and Dad got a job with the Connecticut Leather Company in Hartford. We packed up and moved to a triplex tenement in an all-Jewish neighborhood.

Not long out of high school, my sister Belle married a school chum from Springfield, Massachusetts. George Pollack was a great brother-in-law. He was a baseball umpire trying to get into the major leagues. My sister Marcia then married Sol Feldman, a Hartford man, who played trumpet and was a great musical influence on my life. He was highly respected in the musical community and he helped me immensely in later years.

In 1937, my 16-year-old brother Ben enlisted in the Marine Corps for a four-year hitch. He had no idea that just a few short years later he would be at Pearl Harbor awaiting his discharge on that day that lives in infamy. I was 8 years old when Ben left for boot camp at Paris Island, and I didn't see him again until I was 16.

I was attending Northeast Junior High and hating it. I played hooky as much as possible and was a complete asshole in school. Music was my salvation.

I had been playing with drumsticks since I was about 7 or 8. I had a flair for playing the sticks with the radio. My first pair were furniture dowels that came off the back of a seat we had in the living room. I found that by knocking off the top backrest I could remove the two center pieces, which I thought looked and felt just like drumsticks.

At one point my folks gave me 25 cents to take a lesson with a school teacher, but he was a bore and I only saw him once. I was 11 and attending Hebrew school then, studying for my bar mitzvah. I was also busy joining the drum and bugle brigade across the street at the Catholic parish. The priest in charge was very nice, saw I had some talent and let me use one of their snare drums and march along. None of the kids really read very much and I found that I could fake the marches pretty well. For my 13th birthday my sister Marcia bought me a small set of drums. We had a deaf neighbor with an old, rusty trap set in his garage, consisting of a wood snare, a 28-inch bass drum and a hi-hat pedal with cymbals. One small cymbal was mounted on the bass drum. Marcia paid all of 50 bucks for it, a buck a week out of her secretarial salary.

The State Theater in Hartford was one of the great Big Band theaters in the United States. Fortunately, my father's workplace was right across the street. Every Saturday Mom would fix me a lunch and Dad would take me to work. He would give me my quarter and send me across the street to the State. I would be the first one in line when the box office opened.

In those days you saw an hour stage show at 9 in the morning, then a movie, cartoons and serials for about an hour, then another stage show. Usually the same show as the previous one. It was always a thrill to sit up front and center as the shows began.

The house lights would dim, the famous theme song would start, the curtains would slowly rise as the stage lights came up. I couldn't get enough of it. I felt chills every time I heard "Getting Sentimental Over You" or any of the famous theme songs of those great bands.

There I was, watching every big band of the' 40s– Glenn Miller, Tommy and Jimmy Dorsey, Woody Herman and the Herd, Les Brown, Gene Krupa, Benny Goodman, Lionel Hampton, Artie Shaw, Harry James and all the rest of the bands that came to town, along with popular singers, the famous comedians and vaudeville acts. It was almost as if I were sitting up there with them. I had no idea what an impact they all would have on my later years. I was a 13 and 14-year-old kid during those years and they were probably the happiest of my teenage life– sitting transfixed, glued all day long every Saturday, watching my favorite bands and taking special note of the drummers. I would regretfully leave at 7 at night when my dad got off work.

When we got home, Dad was usually dog-tired and I was full of piss and vinegar. I couldn't wait to get hold of my sticks and run the arrangements I had just heard. I could still smell the theater and the bouquet of the performers' make-up. I just knew that one day the drummer would get sick or fall off the stage and I'd jump up and save the show. How could I miss? I knew all of their arrangements by heart.

When I first set up my drums I set them up backwards. After sitting in the audience and watching these drummers play, I only re-membered that the hi-hat was on my right, etc. I started playing my set as a lefty. My brother-in-law Sol soon straightened me out. He was a handsome dude with a broad smile, and to me he was the epitome of the working musician. He jobbed around town and I remember him wearing a tuxedo, the uniform of the day for musicians. I could hardly wait for my first job and that black bow tie.

Showoff that I was, it wasn't too long before I was setting up my drums on the front porch balcony of our apartment triplex. As soon as I got home from school I would move my drums out onto the porch and serenade all of the kids walking home from school. I was driving the neighborhood nuts. Our landlady lived below us and she was rather ill. Once in the middle of one of my famous porch shows, her husband came up and asked me to stop. She had just passed away. What an awful feeling.

During the fall of 1944 my dad fell gravely ill with asthma. He was told by the doctors that he should leave Connecticut as soon as possible. We lived in a tobacco-growing region, and the asthma was related to the pollen in the air from the tobacco fields. Dad begged, borrowed, and almost signed his life away to get us to California. It was just Mom, Dad and me now. World War II was well under way. Marcia was working and Sol was deferred from military duty while working at Colt Firearms as a .50-caliber machine gun technician.

Our move to California was decided by my sister Belle, who was living in San Bernardino. My mom's sister, Aunt Sarah, was living in Los Angeles and she told Mom that there would be plenty of room for the three of us. So California it was.

Mom went on ahead while Dad and I settled things up in Hartford. We finally got on the train, sitting up in coach along with all of the GIs traveling on leave. Meanwhile, I was dreaming of palm trees and sunshine and all of those movie stars.

2

San Bernardino

Four days and four nights of sitting up on a train traveling across the United States was a great experience for a 14-year-old. I watched soldiers gamble and listened wide-eyed to their overseas experiences. Their stories held me spellbound – hand-to-hand combat, front line stuff. The same kind of action I had seen John Wayne encounter so many times at the State Theater. And my brother over there doing the same thing! Everybody's brothers and fathers were doing the same thing. Such adventure. I couldn't wait to join up.

Of course I was too young, but I knew that I would soon be of age to enlist. It was only a few years later that I was to have my taste of Korea. Then the reality of it all set in. War is bullshit. People die because some goddamn leader of a country decides he wants more power. I often wonder why they don't just send some of those leaders into combat, or better yet just put two of those leaders in the ring and let them fight it out. That would be the end of war in a hurry.

When Dad and I arrived at Union Station in Los Angeles, California was as I had expected. There were palm trees everywhere, some of them actually growing in Union Station. And what a beautiful railroad station it was. Every other station from the East to the West Coast had been dirty and grimy. Engines were still running on coal. Navy men wearing their whites soon looked gray. Our fingernails and hair were always covered with coal soot. But suddenly, here was LA. The sun was shining and everything was so clear. The entire Western atmosphere was clean and sparkling.

This was my first meeting with Aunt Sarah, a lovely robust woman who almost looked like my mother's twin. Sarah's husband, my Uncle L.J. Yolk, was a bald-headed, rather large-nosed man who took charge the minute we arrived, shouting orders at the Red Caps and getting our meager amount of luggage from the baggage compartment.

Our drive in their old Pontiac from downtown Los Angeles, up Wilshire Boulevard, through the Miracle Mile was one of sight and sound. I couldn't have imagined a bigger city in the world. We wound up in the Fairfax District on Clinton Street, in a Spanish style California home. The house was a small tract home, probably 2,000 square feet with three bedrooms, two baths and a one-car garage. It seemed like a palace.

My parents never had a house. We always lived in tenements in a ghetto, where you put dimes and quarters in the gas meter to keep the water hot. We never had a car or a phone. The costs were prohibitive for a poor family. Privacy was something we weren't familiar with either. You could always hear your neighbors going to the bathroom, walking or even fighting. A private home was a totally new experience for me.

L.J. was really a loud hard-ass. He told us what we were going to do. "You're both gonna come to verk in my store. There's plenty verk for everybody!" Mom had already been working there for a few days. Aunt Sarah worked there regularly, and Dad and I were most certainly going to work there also. I guess that was our way of paying for our room and board.

The store was an early version of a supermarket. L.J. had a grocery section, a produce section, and a butcher market with a connecting liquor store and a gigantic parking area in front. L.J. worked my ass off in that store for a couple of weeks until I couldn't handle it anymore. I was ready to run away. Here I was, a frustrated drummer working in a grocery store dragging crates from one end of the store to the other. My dad never complained or argued. He had no backbone as far as I was concerned, but I didn't fully realize our penniless situation. I was rather selfish, getting sick and tired of all of the bullshit L.J. was putting me through. I didn't realize until much later the terrible pressures I created between my folks and L.J..

My uncle didn't understand me – a 14-year-old smoking, for one thing, and then coming home in the evenings after a full day of work and sitting down to a pillow and a pair of drumsticks and practicing for hours at a time. I was a "lazy bum"!

The situation got so unbearable that Dad finally wrote a letter to my sister Belle who was living in San Bernardino, asking her if I could possibly stay with them until things cooled down. She sent a telegram that read: "Plenty of room for Hank, send him down." I was on a bus the next day and the nickname Hank stuck for quite a few years. I hated the name Harold, and Hank was just the sort of nickname that sounded Western and gentile. She, her husband George and their three kids, Art, Howard and Harriet, had to move to California because the children were asthmatics. They had been living in the dry country for a couple of years, in a government housing project called Waterman Gardens.

Sister Belle was the salt of the community. She was always the first one on the block to come to anyone's aid. She was very civic minded, a wonderful lady and a tremendous baseball fan. I moved into the tiny apartment with the five of them and was never happier. This was my new family and I felt a sense of security right away. "The Gardens" had lots of kids to make friends with, and I enrolled in San Bernardino High School, having just turned 15.

All the kids had their own cars in California. In the East you had a car when you were wealthy and had graduated from school. These kids had hot rods and jalopies when they were 15! And they could tear them down and put them back together again. They actually overhauled their own cars. This was magic to me, so I took a part time job at the Mobil station to help out financially, but almost more importantly to learn about cars. I was also introduced to Levis and T-shirts, two fashion trends unheard of at Weaver High in Hartford.

My first day in school I wore my gray blazer and knit tie. I must have looked like a professor or a teacher. I couldn't believe the informality of the school's dress code. Students wore filthy Levis covered with automobile grease and oil. I was also shocked by the number of Mexicans at the school. I had never seen a Mexican before and they were the majority in my classes. I arrived in San Bernardino just about the time it was busting wide open with race riots, part of the Hispanic community riots that spilled out of Los Angeles into the surrounding towns. I was scared to death of any kids who carried knives arid chains and were tattooed with gang codes on their arms and necks.

The first kid I met in The Gardens turned out to become my oldest friend in the world. Bob Kaminski was a big tough Pole from Erie, Pennsylvania. He had just moved to California and we were neighbors in The Gardens. Bob lived with his dad, a plumber. We were exactly the same age, but Bob always considered me older because I was born a few hours before him. He became my mentor, teacher, bodyguard and best friend. Nobody fucked with the Pole from Waterman Gardens. I always felt safe when Bob was around. In no time at all I had started a small band and we were actually working small local jobs for about five bucks a night. Bob had a car and he would drive the band to our jobs and would often sing with us.

He was very mechanically and electrically inclined and taught me about cars and electricity. I guess that's why he never really got into music. In later years he became a plumber and then opened an electrical business.

I fell right into the swing of my new California lifestyle. In 1945 I bought a convertible '28 Dodge Victory Six Roadster with a rumble seat. Bob helped me get it running and we had a ball with that car. We painted the word "Hank" along the entire side of that black car in big white letters with regular paint brushes. It was the talk of the high school. This was a real jalopy compared to the rods the other kids were driving. I guess we were really the laugh of Berdoo High driving around and picking up chicks.

One of my classes at San Bernardino High School was band. I was a drummer, but I couldn't read and this was a pretty advanced music class. I felt like a fool when the teacher introduced me to the rest of the band as a Big Band jazz drummer. Every day this teacher would say, "Okay, pack up." This was our last class of the day and we were almost always five or ten minutes early, but the teacher would make us sit there for those extra minutes. As time went on the kids would just start leaving, filing down a long flight of concrete steps. One day as we were all leaving a few minutes early, the teacher flipped out and started cursing all of us and pushing kids down the steps. The first thing I saw was a girl halfway down the steps with a bloody face. That bastard had gone nuts. I cold-cocked him. I lost control and couldn't hold back.

The next day the police came to our apartment and thank goodness, the officer was a friend of my brother-in-law George. He explained what I had done. That blowout was my major incentive to join the Army. I was turning 16 in a few weeks, so I simply blew town. Bob Kaminski, Bob Steele and Harold Belsky joined up. They were having a "make it a million" drive lowering the enlistment age to 16. We were history.

Korea– The Drummer Boy Goes Overseas

The year was 1946 and I had just turned 16. I really wanted to be like my brother and join the Marines – the few, the proud – but I had heard that at Marine boot camp they threw you off a tower dressed in full field clothing with a hundred-pound pack on your back. You landed in a lake and either swam or sank. I couldn't swim and had a terrible fear of water stemming from a near-fatal accident as a kid in Connecticut. So I went for the Army instead. My folks reluctantly signed my enlistment papers, and I left for basic training with my boyhood pals Bob Kaminski and Bob Steele. We were sent to the engineering base at Fort Lewis, Washington – no place to be in the winter. Along with our introduction to weaponry, survival and military ethics, we also learned to march, salute everything that moved, and function on no sleep at all. We were up every morning at 5, collapsed at about 7 each night, and were awakened at all hours for inspections, forced marches and the general military program for making men out of boys.

Many of the recruits just couldn't cut it. It was a tough grind, but when you're 16 nothing seems insurmountable. If you were in fair shape you could make it through the first couple of months without too much trouble. If you weren't, the Army put you in the best shape of your life.

America was in a patriotic state of mind in the '40s. There were no guys running off to Canada to avoid the draft. We had recently won a war, and all of us felt a sense of duty and obligation to our country. I often had trouble holding back tears as I marched and listened

11

to the brass band blasting out the regimental songs and saw the flags waving.

Our sergeants and officers were all 20-year men just back from combat, and the training was brutal. We kept hearing how tough the front lines were. "We want you guys to live – we lost too many buddies to stupidity. You guys are gonna be the best goddamn outfit in the Army!" My brother had hipped me to many of the scams instructors used to line their pockets. When we were called on to donate money for an iron (so we would be the best uniformed outfit), I knew that it was the same iron used by the last recruits, and probably the ones before them. Next, we needed an ironing board, a coffee pot and on and on. Every few days there was a new scam, and with 55 guys in each barracks trying to kiss ass, it meant 55 bucks for the sergeants, who were already making a good salary. Recruits started out at $40 a month, and these "donations" were bleeding the guys pretty dry. Bob Kaminski, Bob Steele and I never donated. We just never had any money.

My brother had also warned me about volunteering, but I didn't listen. One day the sarge came in and asked if anyone could drive. I was the first guy to raise my hand. He had volunteers follow him to the motorpool, where he quickly assigned us to laundry push-carts. We pushed those carts around for days, picking up dirty laundry while freezing in the snow. Another time a different sergeant came up to me and said, "I understand you're a musician, Belsky." I proudly said yes, just knowing that they needed a drummer somewhere on the base. He handed me a sewing kit and grinned, "Start playing a tune with this!" He had me sewing sheets and blankets for a day.

We finally graduated from basic training and became PFCs. Boy, we had one stripe. We all bought gold engineer insignias (that could pass for captain's bars) at the PX and wore them on our uniforms. They hooked to the collars and lapels of our Ike jackets, and at night we looked like officers strolling around the military post. The new recruits actually saluted us in the dark. We were hot shit.

We were soon ordered to Camp Stoneman in Pittsburg, California, which was the replacement center for men going overseas or for those returning and getting discharged. I was immediately drafted into the base band.

Being a band member, I had a permanent Class A pass, which meant that I could come and go as I pleased at any time of day or night. Most of the men were on "alert" and could get called with an hour's notice to ship out. They rarely even got a pass to go to town.

Bob Steele immediately got his orders and left for the Pacific. We never saw or heard from him again. While Bob Kaminski was waiting for his orders, we were always sneaking out together. We found a concealed water pipeline, one of those gigantic corrugated pipes, and used it regularly to leave the base and head for town.

Then Bob got his orders and left for Japan. That lucky Pole. Everybody wanted orders for Japan – it was like a country club, with easy duty and lots of tme off. Most of the Camp Stoneman replacements were sent off to Japan to join the Army of Occupation.

After a few months our bandleader, Captain Blackburn, was sent overseas. We were assigned a new band captain, and he was strictly military. Every crease in the uniform had to be perfect. We had early morning band marches, and rehearsals all day. It was the pits. I asked for an overseas transfer and got it. My orders: Korea! I had never even heard of Korea.

In mid-November we left the coast of California. It was about 80 degrees, and the sight of San Francisco from the ship was absolutely beautiful. I was sitting back, looking forward to a peaceful ocean cruise. It turned out a little differently than I had planned.

We were 5,500 men on a Liberty troop ship, a Kaiser weld job with the basic four-bunk tiers and a mess hall. Somehow I found myself up on the bridge with a bunch of officers. We all wore dungarees, so no one really knew anybody else's rank. One of the officers asked if I had ever been across before. I said no and he said, "Stick around for the show. As soon as we get under the Golden Gate you can watch the rookies feed the fish." Sure enough, in 20 minutes the railings were lined with soldiers puking their guts out. It really was quite a show. Imagine 5,500 men groaning convulsively and moaning in unison. Well, that wasn't going to happen to me – not much.

I finally found my bunk. I was in compartment 2B, up in the front of the ship, second compartment down. The fore and aft got all of the up and down motion. I was assigned the low bunk, with three men above me. We were literally packed into the compartments like sardines, with hardly any room to move. The stench of sea water and smell of diesel fuel was enough to turn your stomach, and when the ship began to rise and fall, one of the guys started throwing up all over the cabin. The stink was more than anyone could handle, and soon everyone was heaving. I pulled a blanket over me to keep the tossed cookies off. I was sick, but I was determined not to throw up. I could hardly move from the seasickness, but I made up my mind to beat this awful thing.

There was no Dramamine in those days, so you had to get over the seasickness on your own. I often wondered how the soldiers must have felt just a few years before, ordered to invasions with live ammo all around and feeling as bad as we did.

By the third day I felt next to death. The Pacific was roaring. We were cutting into waves 20 feet high. One second the ship was on the top of a swell and the next it was pushed down with a tremendous force of gravity, ten times more than you would feel on an elevator or a carnival ride. The moans and groans in our compartment made it sound like a battlefield hospital. Everyone wanted to die. I hadn't eaten for several days, except for sucking an orange and eating a candy bar. I was still dressed in my dungarees, with my boots on, just lying there watching the slop wash from one end of the cabin to the other while the ship plowed into wave after wave. I couldn't remember a worse time in my life, and I wondered how I could survive another 30 days. That afternoon, a work detail entered our compartment and started hosing down everyone and everything. A riot almost broke out, and the MPs were called to break it up. Everyone's nerves were worn to a frazzle. You couldn't look at a guy without getting a, "What the fuck are you looking at, asshole?" as the vomit came out of his mouth like it was shot from a fire hose. The officer in charge ordered us all to get up and go out on deck. The fresh air felt good and the sea had calmed down a bit. I started to feel a little better.

Somehow we got through the initial ordeal and then the hunger pangs started to hit. I knew that I had to get some food. The officers told us to eat, shave, shower, and get shipshape. I started feeling confident that I was going to be all right.

I entered the mess hall filled with men either waiting in line or standing up at the counters eating lunch. The sea was relatively calm, and we were below decks about midship, where there was less motion. Occasionally, a guy would run from the hall, heading for the railing. With steel tray in hand, I waited my turn in line. One guy slapped a gob of mashed potatoes on your tray, the next poured some gravy, then another spooned out some peas, com, and so on.

The guy in front of me asked for more com, and the galley slave told him to shove off. The guy jumped over the counter and grabbed the galley slave by the throat and the fight was on. The entire mess hall broke out in a brawl, a full-blown riot. The MPs rushed in once again to break it up and restore law and order. Everyone was in a state of hate.

I finally got my entree, a greasy hamburger steak, and headed for an open spot. I squeezed in between two guys and started eating. I was nearly starved and it tasted pretty good. We all stood side by side and faced the guys on the other side of the stand-up counter. Nobody sat. The tables were just above waist high and just wide enough to hold your tray and the guy's across from you. Ten guys stood at each table, five on each side facing each other. Just as I started chowing down on my first food in days, the guy facing me opened his mouth and out shot the vomit, covering me and my food. I headed for a ladder and up to a spot on the railing as fast as my feet could move. I had the dry heaves for the next few hours and a raging headache that made me wish I were dead. But by the end of the day I somehow got my sea legs and wasn't sick again for the rest of the voyage.

As we approached the Korean coastline the snow was falling heavily. The ship dropped anchor and we were transferred to LSTs, Navy landing vessels. There was no dock in Inchon Harbor large enough to handle big ships. It was mid-December.

After making it to shore, we froze our asses off waiting for the narrow-gauge railroad that would take us to the repo depot. We spent a few hours on the train, packed together like cattle, trying to stay warm. There were no windows or floor center, most of us were assigned tents to bunk in. The only covered buildings were a few old Japanese barracks. I was lucky enough to get assigned to one of these small buildings. As filthy as it was, with just a few mattresses covered with soot and grime, slept on by God-only-knows how many thousands of GIs before me, I felt fortunate to have a roof over my head instead of freezing in a canvas tent.

There were five troop ships in, with over 5,000 men each. That meant more than 25,000 soldiers waiting for assignments. The word was that everyone would be going into infantry outfits. Real soldiering.

Can you imagine 25,000 men lining up for chow? Standing on sheet ice, freezing in a line that seemed endless – it was so cold that when you put your utensils into the vat of boiling water and chemicals for sterilization and then pulled them out, you would hear a click as they instantly froze. No one bathed or shaved for days.

After three or four days of sitting in a gigantic warehouse and listening to names being called for assignments, an officer came in and made a speech. "The next six guys that I call are the luckiest bastards to ever hit Korea. You're going to steam-heated barracks with hot showers and breakfast the way you like it every morning." I knew he wasn't talking to me, so I sat back and ignored the whole thing. The first name called was "Belsky, Harold S. RA 192 444 77." The six of us picked up our gear and,were driven to our "country club." I didn't know what was going on, but I didn't open my mouth. No infantry for me, thank God. All I could think of was the big sign that had welcomed us all to Korea, the first thing we had seen as we got off the LSTs: "Welcome to Inchon, the best damn port in the Pacific." What a laugh.

When we arrived at our destination, the 657th Compound, we were greeted by a group of officers, soldiers and Korean civilians who picked up our gear and escorted us to a real military barracks. It was actually a converted Japanese factory, with long hallways and skylights running the length of the building and private rooms on either side. The friendliness of the guys and the warmth of the barracks was an incredible change from the previous month. It was wonderful.

We were each assigned a separate room – I couldn't believe what was happening. We had just left thousan:ds of GIs sleeping in tents, and here I was, the boy drummer from Holyoke, being put up in a Hilton. We were shown the shower rooms and the mess hall and then were told that dinner would be in an hour. "If you're not hungry, just go to sleep for a couple of days. You'll get a wake-up call." .

The hot shower was heaven. The last time I had showered had been two weeks before, aboard the ship. Those awful steel showers were cold, with very little hot water and all of it salty seawater. Showering aboard troop ships with special saltwater soap was the worst. You itched for days.

After showering, I headed for my room and covered myself with a big olive drab blanket marked "US. Army." I awoke the next day around noon to find a young man hanging up my clothes and cleaning my room. He was a Korean boy about my age and spoke almost no English. He pointed at himself and said, "Me Kim." As I got out of bed, he handed me a bathrobe and opened the door so I could go to the latrine. I was speechless.

I asked a couple of guys about Kim. They informed me that we each had houseboys. Kim was a student, working to help his family.

He was also saving up to get married. Kim did all the dirty work. He had worked through the night, washing my clothes and pressing my uniforms. The salary was meager, so I was told to give a tip now and then – a toothbrush, a carton of cigarettes, an old shirt.

I spent the next hour or so walking all over the compound. We had all the special military equipment an engineering base would need. We were surrounded by an 8-foot wall that encompassed the

12-acre base. It had a main gate for entry and a few side gates with 24-hour guards keeping an eye on the heavy equipment and surveying gear. The roads were all dirt, as were the streets surrounding us on the outside. It was like a small town just outside of Seoul. The base didn't seem very busy, and I began to wonder what my job was. I soon found out.

After a late lunch, the six of us were sent to Major Brooks' office. We were congratulating each other on our fortunate assignment when the door popped open; we snapped to attention and saluted the major. He saluted us back and said, "Please sit down, gentlemen." Major Brooks was a mild-mannered man with blondish hair, about 35 years old. He wore his shirt open with no tie – a bit casual for a company commander.

"We don't stand on military formality here," he told us, "Nobody salutes, nobody jumps to attention. We're all on a first name basis. You guys were picked because of your college educations in geodetic surveying, airborne photography and mapmaking skills. We're in the midst of using aerial photography to remap Korea below the 38th Parallel. It isn't the easiest job in the world, but it sure beats the hell out of infantry duty." I knew instantly that a big mistake had been made. I could already see myself packing up and saying goodbye to my country club. What a drag. As Major Brooks looked over the records of each man, spouting engineering terms I had never heard before, all I could feel was a lump in my stomach. As he interviewed each man and assigned him to the appropriate job, he kept picking up my M.O.S. military work sheet, flicking it with his finger, putting it down and picking up the next man's sheet. The other five were sent off to offices, map rooms, dark room facilities or lens shops. I was left sitting there alone with the Major.

He picked up my records once again and glanced at them. "Well, Belsky, it certainly looks like a mistake has been made. I see that you're just out of basic training, no college education, and you don't really have a military occupation yet. It looks like you're gonna have to go back to the repo depot for another assignment. I'm very sorry."

I slowly got to my feet and nodded. Then he glanced down again at my records and said, 'just a second. I see here that you play the drums. Are you a professional?" "Yes, sir, more or less," I replied.

"Well, we've got another musician here, too. Let me give him a call." He cranked. the phone and asked for Santy. A moment later he said, "Santy, we've got a drummer down here that was sent over with the new batch. Why don't you come down and talk to him?" Lieutenant Santos came running in, out of breath. "Jesus, we need a drummer – you must have been sent from heaven!" Santos was a trumpet player from Boston, Massachusetts. Since I had grown up in nearby Connecticut, we were practically neighbors, especially when you found yourself on the other side of the world. He was genuinely excited and explained that they had an all-officer band and no drummer.

"Can you type?" he asked.

"Not really." "Can you drive a car?" he inquired hopefully.

"Yes, sir!" "Okay, Belsky, you're gonna be my jeep driver and you're gonna learn how to type. I'll have you assigned to my office."

It was the beginning of a great friendship and quite a learning experience. I did learn how to type, but we spent so much time away from the base on field trips that I felt like I was in summer camp. Santos requisitioned a full set of white Gretsch drums and Zildjian cymbals, which arrived in two weeks from Japan. Here was this Jewish PFC drummer playing with an all-officer band. We played at all the officers' clubs, parties and special events. When we weren't playing as a full band, we played as trios and various combinations, and they always needed drums.

Each morning we gathered in the dining room and Sergeant Ching cooked our breakfast the way we wanted it. Fresh eggs. Plenty of milk and juice. Our unit of 65 men was drawing rations for 300. At the time, the Air Force was flying missions over Korea to collect photographs for our survey operations. The new photos arrived every morning, along with the fresh rations. We took the aerial photographs and studied them under a stereoscope, noting landmarks and then finding their actual locations in the field. We then made pin pricks on the photos and sent them back to Japan for further processing and assembling for maps.

My duties were to drive Santos and the other officers through the mountains and help set up the stereoscope equipment. They would do the pin pricking and surveying, and we'd drive off to another landmark. It was usually a 9-to-5 day, an easy job and plenty of driving and fresh air. When I wasn't out in the field, I typed reports to accompany the photographs. And once a month, I pulled 24-hour guard duty, which everyone had to do.

My first field trip was certainly a memorable one. Four of us drove about 30 miles from the base and found a hill to survey. The other three took off over the hills and left me alone in the jeep with a box of sandwiches and a case of Ballantine ale. The ale was packed in a 24-can corrugated box, totally covered with wax for overseas shipping. These cases were a bitch to open. You had to do a lot of digging with a knife to cut through all the packing.

Korea was known for jeep stripping. We were constantly advised to never leave a jeep unattended because the North Koreans were everywhere and would rob you blind if they got the chance. And murder was not unusual. This was my first trip to the field, and I hadn't even been assigned my .45 or carbine. I was just sitting there alone in the peaceful countryside when I was suddenly surrounded by about 30 Koreans. They appeared from nowhere and they were angry. They started rocking the jeep, and I figured I was going to die right there. I was so scared that all I could think to do was grab the case of Ballantine. With superhuman strength I tore open the case and pulled out a few of the shiny gold cans. I raised them over my head and started screaming like a madman. The North Koreans thought they were grenades and scattered. I fired up the jeep and tore off. That night I got my rifle and my .45 and was never without them.

After my tour of duty in Korea I got orders to ship out. I was in a panic about going back on another cattle boat, but was fortunate to get assigned to a presidential liner. As soon as I cleared the deck, I looked up the officer in charge and volunteered my services as a band member. He took me to a small stateroom and said, "You're the first to volunteer – you'll be the bandleader." I had my own stateroom with an electric fan and a private shower.

When we arrived back at Camp Stoneman for discharge, we were put into field barracks and told to sit tight. The next day an officer came by for a "friendly" chat.

"Confidentially, men, it's gonna take quite some time to process all of your discharge papers. As you know, there are thousands of you waiting. Now, any of you men that want to join the reserves will be discharged within a day. That's the way they're doing it. The rest of you will probably have to spend a couple of weeks waiting around. It's up to you." There was no way I was going to join anything. I settled in for the long wait, but we were discharged within a couple of days. Our confidential officer buddy was, of course, full of shit. Then I was off to San Bernardino and a family reunion.

4

Chicago

After I was discharged from the Army in 1948, I started traveling with various groups and settled in with a "funny hat" band called The Novelteers, also known as the Stan Moore Trio. Stan played sax, Keith Curtiss played piano and I was on drums. I MC'd, sang and we did comedy. We created pantomime bits for popular records and were doing quite well on the road.

We traveled to Alaska and worked the Talk of the Town in Fairbanks. Talk about tough. These were the pre-Statehood days. The waiters were all men – tough Alaskan types, ex-cons and the like. When there was a fight, it was a John Wayne movie-type fight. No one gave up until someone was knocked out or dead. If the loser was dead, he was covered with a tarp and not moved. until the commissioner arrived from Juneau.

This was the Northern territory, and the Alcan Highway was being built at the time. Summer was three months long and the sun shined 24 hours a day. The construction men worked as many hours a day as possible, earning somewhere in the neighborhood of a thousand bucks a day.

Our audiences consisted mostly of men – construction men out for a good time. Here we were wearing dresses and falsies and silly hats doing pantomime and trying our best to entertain these gorillas. In retrospect, you could say that it was great show biz basic training. Every now and then a female singer would be booked to work for a week or two and we would back her. These girls would come in with 17-piece band arrangements and here we were with only a piano, sax and drums – not even a bass to fill it up. But even with the problems, just about every singer would tell me how much they liked the way I "accompanied" them.

That was a key word that stuck with me all through the years. "Accompanist." I was very fortunate to learn early on that my role was to be an accompanist.

When the summer of 1948 rolled over and the nights got longer and colder we closed Fairbanks and headed for the States. We worked every kind of dump imaginable and wound up in a club called Tommy's Ranch House in Great Falls, Montana. During our touring, I had my first real love affair in Medford, Oregon, with an older woman (I was 18). She broke off our relationship to go back with her ex-husband, something I couldn't figure out because he supposedly beat her mercilessly and consequently was in jail when we met. She went back to him and I went traveling with my heart in a sling. In a way, this torrid love affair that turned out so bad led to a good move on my part.

I often remembered the movie *Young Man With A Horn*. I cried like a baby seeing this poor dude in a montage of nightclub ramblings, drunk out of his head. Unfortunately, there I was doing the same thing. I started drinking like a loony and hardly knew what I was doing or where I was. I was calling this woman and she was never in. When she was, she would tell me to stop calling her. That New Year's Eve in Great Falls, Montana, with the snow falling and the temperature around 40 degrees below zero, was a night that I will never forget. I was merrily drinking my way into oblivion, and that's all I remember until I woke up around 5 a.m.

Tommy's Ranch House had been a health club originally until it became a nightclub. There was a full basement with little green rooms and massage tables in each room. I woke up on one of those tables in the center of this tiny green room, and I just knew that I was in the city morgue. The walls were wet with sweat from the cold and I was shivering uncontrollably. I started screaming for help – for an attendant to come get me out. I wasn't dead, that I was sure of, but at the same time all I could think of was that some doctor was going to come in and start an autopsy on me. That was the end of my drinking.

In 1949, I was just turning 20 when my buddy Rick Verdi talked me into going to Chicago to study at the Roy C. Knapp School of Percussion. I had been traveling all over the country with The Novelteers, working every kind of crumb dump imaginable. Chicago sounded great, and it was. I moved in with Rick and his immigrant parents, and I lived with them for a few weeks until I found a small room over a garage on the West Side.

I enrolled immediately, and just as fast felt the history of this school encompassing my every thought. There were about 500 drummers of all ages studying with various teachers – great, dedicated teachers. This was the first time I felt a sense of being with "names;" people like the old man Roy Knapp (who personally taught Gene Krupa, one of my idols), Bob Tilles, Bob Seaman and the late Hugh Anderson. (I had the pleasure of working with Hugh in later years in Hollywood.) Jose Bethancourt, part of the NBC staff orchestra in Chicago at that time, was teaching marimba. I was minoring in piano and vibes.

The Knapp School was composed of all types of people, from young kids to older professionals, with quite a few boxers, who were studying independent coordination. Independent coordination was the latest thing for a drummer to study, and many fighters were studying how to throw a punch while stepping back or getting the next hand ready to throw.

Classes consisted of every kind of musical training – music appreciation, harmony, arranging, sight singing and reading, drums, all of the percussion instruments and lots of homework. I was fortunate enough to be able to handle a full curriculum, thanks to Uncle Sam. I was taking advantage of my GI Bill before it ran out.

School started at 8 a.m. and went to 5 p.m., with a break for lunch. I would ride the El (subway) from the West Side to downtown Chicago and back every day. I soon got tired of the long commute and talked to my dad about some financial help. He agreed to help pay some toward my room. I took a room in the Majestic Hotel in the Loop, just a few blocks from school. Now I had much more time to study and play drums.

The old Majestic Hotel was the cheapest hotel in the Loop. It was sleaze personified. In the early 1900s it had been one of the finer hotels in Chicago, but by 1949 it was the pits! It had about 12 floors and was considered a high-rise in the old days, one little accordioned-door elevator that took forever, and a penthouse ballroom that hadn't been used for about 50 years. It was covered with cobwebs and echoed like thunder. I was investigating the ballroom one afternoon and discovered an old grand piano under a bunch of junk. It became my practice piano.

The Majestic was populated by hookers, pimps, addicts, pushers, gangsters and strippers. Chicago was a mecca for burlesque houses and "bust out" strip joints. Strippers would do their strip act and then come down into the audience and "mix" with the customers. The customer would buy a drink for the lady, and the lady would quickly drink it (it was almost always plain tea) and keep the swizzle stick that came with the water chaser. After an evening of work these girls (called B girls) usually accumulated 30 or 40 of these sticks and would trade them in for 50 cents a piece. If the sucker bought champagne at 25 bucks a bottle, she would get about five bucks. We used to break up onstage watching some poor slob jerk off under the table while he was watching some lovely thing, practically naked except for a G-string and a couple of pasties, dance on stage. The guys never realized that anyone knew, being so cool about it. Chicago was a convention town and there was always something going on. It was still loaded with syndicate, and they seemed to run the town. Most cops seemed to be "on the take."

I was told always to have a couple of bucks paper-clipped to my license, and when a cop asked for it just hand it to him. He would hand it back without the money and you would drive away. That wasn't done in L.A., pal; you'd go straight to jail. One night after Rick Verdi and his wife Mary had just been married, they called and said they were going for pizza. They wanted me along. I jumped into the beautiful Buick that Rick had recently purchased and settled in the back seat. Rick had been drinking pretty good before they picked me up, and after we finished our meal with more wine, Rick had even more booze. He wasn't a drinker, but this night he was celebrating.

About 2 a.m., with the snow falling like crazy and the roads as slick as could be, Rick ran a red light. Suddenly, a cop was chasing us with red lights and siren blasting. Rick refused to stop. Mary and I screamed for him to stop but he was pissed and refused. Soon there were a couple more cars chasing us, and I just knew that they'd start shooting any second. I laid down on the floorboards, like I had seen in movies, hoping they would miss. I knew I was going to be killed in a hail of police bullets.

We were running every goddamn light on the West Side, sliding all over the trolley tracks. It was a real chase scene. We finally came to a wall of black and whites with drawn guns, red lights flashing and murder on their faces. About nine police cars circled us. Rick casually got out of the car and walked up to the policemen who were lining up. He started handing out ten dollar bills. They patiently waited their turn, and as they each received a bill they would say thank you very courteously and walk out of line. I wouldn't have believed it if I hadn't seen it with my own sober eyes.

Rick calmly waved and yelled a couple of thank yous and got back in the car and they drove me home. It was plain luck that Rick had just been paid and was carrying that bundle with him. It was a real scary experience.

After about a year of attending the Knapp School I started to get calls from various leaders to do casuals. Don Knapp, Roy's son, got to know me as a student and started sending me on some of his lesser jobs. Then I started getting strip joint calls. Ju-Ju's Glass Show Lounge on the west side and the 606 Club on South State, and some of the Rush Street joints like Minsky's Burlesque Theater. I would sub for regular drummers and was getting some great sightreading experience.

That reading experience really paid off. One night while sitting in my hotel room I got a call from a stripper who was a neighbor in the hotel. She was calling from the Post Time Club, about ten blocks away on North State Street. Their drummer had taken ill and could I come right over and get on the drums? I sure could.

Piano, trumpet and drums. From 8 p.m. to 4 a.m. with no intermissions. If you had to hit the toilet you switched instruments. The shows consisted of a comic coming out and doing a few minutes, then a stripper would come out and do her three numbers – slow, medium and fast. During the slow number I would get on the piano and the piano man could go to the toilet, and if I had to go to the toilet the trumpet player would get on the drums for the slow number. Of course, the trumpet player could go anytime he needed. That was the way it went all night. Comic, dancer, comic, dancer.

We had special red lights over the bandstand. If they ever flashed on and off quickly for a few seconds, it was a signal from the doorman that we were to go immediately into a fast two-beat version of "Billboard." This let the girls know that the vice squad was entering the joint and they would grab whatever clothing they had shed and run off the stage. The comic would run on stage and start a gag in the middle and deliver a phony punchline. The audience was always wise to what was going on. The girls were stripping much too much clothing according to the law in those days, and they were never to be caught in an undressed mode. Of course the doormen knew all of the vice cops who were on the take and we had plenty of forewarning. But this was a new experience for me.

I finished that first night, and one of the bosses called me into a small office. He handed me some cash and asked me if I could work again the next night if their regular drummer couldn't make it. I said sure and that was that. I had to be to school in a matter of a few hours. It was about 4:30 in the morning.

When I finished school the next day and got back to my hotel room there was a note from the club. Come to work. Again I worked the same routine and it was great. There were about eight or nine girls in the show, all gorgeous strippers. I would walk into the dressing room, which was the only way to the stage, and all of the girls would be sitting around nude or semi-nude. Someone would yell, "Who the hell are you?" And they'd all cover themselves. I told them I was the drummer, and they'd all drop their clothing and go back to their make-up or whatever. Boy, those were tough nights.

At the close of that second night, the boss called me into his office again and introduced himself as Tony. He was a rugged looking man built like a small bull, with a huge chest and arms like vise grips. He explained that Mickey Scrima (ex-Harry James drummer through-out the 1940s and one of my favorites) was not returning to the Post Time Club.

"Have you got a set of drums kid?" he asked in his broken Italian accent. "I sure do!" I replied. He asked me if I smoked any of those crazy cigarettes or if I drank, and I told him I didn't. He told me that he would start me at a hundred a week. (Seven days a week.) Tough hours, but boy, what money in those days. I was thrilled.

After about a week at the club, Tony called me into his little office one night; I was afraid that I had done something wrong. On the contrary, he told me that all of the girls loved the way I played for them, that I had a good feel for their music and that he also liked me and my sober ways. He raised my salary to a hundred and a quarter and made me the bandleader. I was honored. He also drew open a curtain, and lo and behold, there was a beautiful set of drums. His. He was a hobby drummer and wanted some pointers.

Needless to say, we became very good friends for the two years I worked there. Tony would take me home on Sundays and treat me to his family-style Sunday dinners. It was like being in Italy. About 20 people would sit around a huge dining room table. Tony and his wife and mother and father, all of the brothers and sisters and a few friends thrown in. These were happy times for me. But there were also sad times. I had gotten mixed up with some very tough people – leg breakers – that were part of the "outfit." I was a member of local 10 at that time in Chicago, and some people were giving me a bad time. Tony made one call and I never heard from these people again.

In 1951 I completed my Knapp training. Now I had to go out into the world and face the future. I decided to head for L.A. Studios were calling to me, but I didn't know it yet.

I returned to "Berdoo" as the locals call San Bernardino, much wiser and a much better-schooled musician. I joined Joe New-man, the piano player from South America, and spent a few years at the Magic Carpet in Berdoo. The Magic Carpet was a local supper club owned by Ken Berry, a wonderful, rotund organist. Ken decided to completely remodel the club and bring in semi-name acts. I guess I got more sight-reading experience there than anywhere except for the strip clubs in Chicago. It was at the Magic Carpet that I met and became friendly with Lenny Bruce. I met Lenny in front of the club on his opening day. I was waiting for Ken to come along and open the club for a rehearsal with the new act that week. Lenny drove up and parked in front of the club. He was driving the most beat-up old Dodge or Plymouth coupe that I had ever seen. The upholstery was all ripped up as if a cat had torn it to shreds. The fenders were all crunched and the car had about a year's din and grime on it. Lenny got out of the car and walked to the trunk and opened it. He saw me staring at the car and didn't know who I was from Adam. I didn't know who he was, either. He looked directly at me and said: "This is really a Porsche, man, but I hate the body styles!" We became friends from that day until his untimely death. He asked me if I was a Jewish kid, and when I said yes he handed me a confidential magazine that he had over-pasted every line, including headlines, with Yiddish writings from the *Forward Jewish* newspaper. I knew that this guy was a genius. He kept me laughing for two weeks straight, day and night. We used to drive to the mountains every other day (Lake Arrowhead and Big Bear). When his car finally busted, I would drive him to L.A., where he lived on La Brea Avenue near Melrose above a store. He was living like a pauper.

I was driving a rather new Mercury Sun Valley in those days. I bought it from a fireman. It was fire engine red and had a white leather interior and a continental kit on the back. It was a sharp car, and it had a Plexiglas bubble top. While driving Lenny to L.A. one night, he was leaning back and looking up at his reflection in the glass top. The green Plexiglas combined with the green dash lights produced a strange green glow. It was an eerie sight. "Look man, when I die I'm gonna look just like this in my coffin–" That was really the sick humor of Lenny Bruce...

On opening night when Lenny was introduced, we played a fanfare and Lenny walked out to a respectable burst of applause. (San Bernardino was not known for its sense of humor, and a few drunken military types were sitting ringside.) "Hi folks. Look, I'm an Italian movie star!" He was holding a big piece of hair under his armpit. "Ha, ha, ha!" came a very sarcastic reply from a soldier. Lenny answered without skipping a beat, "Ha, ha, ha, your ass!" Dirty words were just never used at the Magic Carpet. The audience screamed, as did the soldiers. Lenny was their kind of guy. They loved him. So did we. During my stint at the Magic Carpet, a local ordinance was passed stating that all nightclubs had to have a peace officer on duty while a band was playing. Ken Berry asked if anyone owned a gun. I did. Ken said "You're gonna be a cop." He wasn't about to have to pay a cop to guard the place while the band played. He checked with the local D.A. and asked if one of the band members could be sworn in. That would save him another salary. I was sworn in and became a special police officer for the city of San Bernardino. I actually had a badge and an old pistol.

When we first started at the Carpet there was a female singer in the band. Her name was Vicki Young. She was a buxom blonde and sang great. The audiences loved her, and in no time she was signed to Capitol Records. Voyle Gilmore was producing Vicki. We were all happy for her because this was her big break. Little did I know that this would be the turning point in my musical career.

Vicki was one-quarter Oklahoma Cherokee Indian. She was from a musical family that toured Oklahoma and played all of the country dumps in the West. Her father retired from the music business and took up residence in Berdoo. He was a workman at Norton Air Base. Her mother was a salesperson at a local magic tricks and hobby shop. They were sweet people. As countrified as people could be. Her name was Mintie and his name was Lodi. The Stegalls. They lived in a shack at the foothills of the San Bernardino mountains, a shack always covered with an inch of dust from the blowing thermals that swept down from the mountains. Vicki and her baby sister Karen lived with the folks and Vicki's little boy, Gary. Vicki's signing with Capitol meant that one hit record could put them all on easy street.

Vicki and I started dating. She was beautiful and I really fell for her. I was still pretty young. Vicki was a few years older. She would let me escort her to recording dates in Hollywood at the old Capitol recording studios. Now I got to watch Dave Cavannaugh conduct the Big Bands, and here I was feeling the way I did during the old

State Theater days in Hartford. I knew this was for me. Vicki tried to get me on some of her sessions, but Voyle wouldn't have any part of an inexperienced "husband-drummer." He was right. I really wasn't ready, and thank God I didn't do any of those sessions, because I could have blown my career. Working onstage or in clubs is one thing, but when it comes to the studios, you better have some demo experience because of the high costs of studio time. They always remember the guy that screwed up, as well as the guy that helped make a hit.

Vicki's recordings of *Tweedle De Dee* and *Ricochet Romance* started making some noise. She had to go on the road and I was ready. I loved to travel, and I naturally became Vicki's drummer and some-time conductor. We went to Hawaii in 1952 when Hawaii was still comparatively native. We worked all over the country and it was a ball. And I was getting more Big Band experience.

On the return from one of our trips (I had a small apartment in a garage in San Berdoo,) Vicki called me one morning and asked me to come to the house quickly. I rushed over and found the family very upset. Little Gary had taken ill. I called a local doctor and he came immediately. He sent the boy off to the hospital and little Gary was put in isolation, in an iron lung, suffering from polio. (This was just a couple of months before the Salk vaccine announcement.) We stayed at the hospital all day watching that tiny boy in the iron lung, and we felt so helpless. About 4 that afternoon the doctor walked up to us and informed us that Gary had died. After the screaming and the wailing had subsided, the doctor took me aside thinking that I was the father and said, "You and your wife have another baby right away." The next few days were horrible. The family bereaved like I had never seen before. It seemed like the end of the world. Vicki was scheduled to open in Vegas in a few days, and she was going to cancel. I talked her into working and added, "Let's get married." We were married in Vegas and were pretty happy for a while. But, as so many marriages go, we soon realized that we were not really compatible. Our lifestyles were totally opposite. We very quietly got divorced, and Vicki soon married someone else and gave up her career.

Not long after Vicki and I were divorced, I found myself visiting my brother Ben in Lake Tahoe. He was a dealer at the Sahatis Country Club (later to become Harrah's.) I took refuge and he got me a job at Sahatis as a shill. The year was 1958 and I was sort of drifting, group after group and band after band. I walked into Sahatis one night and spotted a female dealer at the roulette wheel. She looked about 19 years old and was pregnant. She was absolutely beautiful. So striking.

29

A brunette about 5 feet 10. I went on about my business, and later that night was sitting with a gang of dealers and musicians who were talking about Joy, the roulette dealer. They were talking about the rough deal she had gotten from some guy that was supposed to marry her and than ran off with his ex-wife or something. She seemed like she was about to commit suicide. She hated being in that condition and hated the fact that she had lost the man she adored.

I had just joined the Carol Simpson Group at Sahatis after quitting the Extroverts. The next night I walked up to Joy, introduced myself, and asked her to marry me and come to L.A. with me and the group. She just knew that I must be crazy. We were married the next day and Joy came to L.A. She didn't want the child, and we arranged for a private adoption. Joy and I moved into a small apartment and we were living a quiet, happy life. I was now traveling quite a bit, and we weren't seeing as much of each other as we would have liked, but that was show biz and she was wonderful about it.

I phoned Joy one night and she mentioned that her mother, who was living in Las Vegas, asked her to come up for a visit. I thought that was great and she did. During that stay she met Jane Russell, who offered to get her a job at the Tropicana Hotel. Joy asked my opinion, and I told her to jump at the chance. She really didn't want to do it, but I finally convinced her. She did, and became one of the most beautiful showgirls in Las Vegas. She never had to do any nude stuff. Just stand and look gorgeous. And she was.

I would fly into Vegas every chance I had, and we would really enjoy our get-togethers. Joy was rooming with Felicia, another of the beautiful showgirls, and everything was just rosy. My travels were now keeping me away longer and longer, and I couldn't help feeling that this was no life for Joy. She wanted only to be a homemaker, and this show biz stuff was getting to her.

I was working in Canada, and my band was spending the day on a beautiful yacht on Lake Ontario when the ship-to-shore phone rang. It was Joy. The Tropicana Hotel had entered her in the Miss Nevada contest. Joy had just become Miss Nevada, but she wasn't a Miss. So the Tropicana attorneys talked to me about a quiet divorce and then a quiet remarriage after things got back to normal. Joy was going for the Miss Universe contest. She was against the divorce, but again I convinced her that this was a perfect move on her part. The hotel stood to get millions of dollars worth of publicity, and it would help her eventually too. I know that Joy loved me in her own way, and I certainly loved her too, but I couldn't help but feel that Joy's real love was actually gratitude to a guy who came along and sort of saved her from ruination. The hotel took care of everything, sent a courier with the papers and we were divorced. No muss, no fuss.

5

Tommy Sands

The endless touring continued, and in 1957 I was working with a nondescript comedy band traveling all over the United States. I was doing jokes, MCing and playing my drums. We would work Duluth, Minnesota, in February and Tucson, Arizona, in August. We would travel from one end of the U.S. to the other to work for five days, only to find out that we had to go back again. Another 3,000 mile drive. These days were among the lowest for me. But then, almost magically, the leader informed our little co-op band (we all shared and shared alike, moneywise) that our seven-piece group would finally be going to Las Vegas, that magical town, where working in a lounge meant a shot at the big time. After months of being financed by our singer, Shirley Claire, and barely eking out a living, this was like a dream come true.

We opened at the Golden Nugget in downtown Vegas. The crowds liked our music, and we felt pretty good about the group. We all earned around two hundred and fifty bucks a week. After the scant money we had been making, this really felt like the big time. When our first payday rolled around, we all huddled in the small office of the paymaster, our illustrious leader, ready for the big bucks. Crying and bellowing, he informed us that he had gambled the entire payroll away at the tables. Shock, disbelief, horror and then murder entered our minds simultaneously.

Sometimes a bad experience can lead to a good one. In this case something good did come out of the horror story. The owners let us all draw cash in advance, we finished our few weeks there and were booked at Harvey's Wagon Wheel in Lake Tahoe, Nevada. This was another great lounge for showcasing funny hat bands, and these jobs usually led to bigger and better things. Again we opened to a great crowd and did a rousing first set. We were back on Cloud Nine.

When I had visited my brother at Lake Tahoe a few years earlier, I had become friendly with other dealers, pit bosses, security men and the like who worked at the hotels and casinos at the lake. Felix was one such boss.

As we came off stage after our opening show at Harvey's Wagon Wheel, a hand grabbed me and whirled me around. It was Felix and he was obviously happy to see me. I had at times hung around the Wagon Wheel Lounge while working at Sahatis, and often sat in with Ian Bernard and his group. Ian, a great pianist and composer, was making a big name for himself in television and movies.

Felix said, "Well kid, you're making the big bucks, I'm proud of ya!"

"Well," I said, "Three hundred and fifty bucks a week is better than a poke in the eye with a stick, but I wouldn't exactly call it the big bucks." Boy, was I wrong. Felix took me up to the office and showed me a contract for about $7,000 a week. Now, we were a coop band, a band making equal money. What a laugh! I was supposed to be making around a thousand a week, and our bum bandleader was obviously taking all the money. That's all I had to see.

In seconds I was on the bandstand packing my drums. On my way out, a young Latin-looking guy said, "Hey, what are ya doin'?"

"I'm splitting man;' I said. "I've been had and now I've had it up to here!"

"How about joining my group next door at Harrah's Lounge?" he said. "It's just a small casino, but we're going to open in Hollywood in a couple of weeks. My drummer got sick and we could really use you." It was an opponunity I couldn't pass up. "Grab a case!" I shouted, "and let's go!"

My drums were set up in nothing flat, and that was the start of my tenure with the Carol Simpson Quartet. Now I was playing out-and-out jazz, my love of the day. Our first stop was the Garden of Allah in Hollywood, the jazz lounge noted for all the movie stars, producers and the like. I knew this would be the stepping stone to a studio career.

I was on top of the world, working every night at the Garden and playing for the Hollywood crowd. It was the kind of job I had dreamed of getting. Carol was as pretty as ever, her fingers rolling over the piano like waves on the ocean, Rocky playing a great conga line and our bassist was just groovin'. Ours was a happy group, and it was nice to be appreciated again. Rocky and Carol had a great apartment on Romaine near the Garden, and they put me up until 1 found my own place. We were planning to settle in to a good steady job.

One night, just about closing time, a man walked up to me and said, "I like the way you play, kid. I got a hot job for you." It turned out that he was the personal manager for a country group called The Raiders, and they were working at a little dump out in Bell, California. These kids were neighbors of Tommy Sands.

Tommy was on his way to becoming America's teenage idol, after Elvis, of course, who was in the service at the time. Elvis' infamous manager, Colonel Tom Parker, knew Tommy and Tommy's mother, Grace, from their Houston days. When the Kraft Theatre did a special called "The Singing Idol," Elvis was all set to do it, but his military stint interrupted the show and Colonel Tom called Tommy to do it. Tommy was a DJ in Houston at the time, and he jumped at the chance. The show was a smash and Tommy was an overnight star. Thousands of letters poured into NBC and all the record companies were after Tommy. He eventually signed with Capital and recorded *Teenage Crush*. Now Tommy needed a band.

Tommy had inadvertently heard these kids practicing in a room at a hotel across the street from his house on South Rossmore, and he became interested in the group. He told them that he was looking for a backup band, but that they would have to find a drummer. Their manager told me that I could make some really big money – the group was booked all over the world. Was I interested? No. I didn't know a thing about rock and roll or country, and rockabilly seemed to be their thing. The manager came back the next night and offered me a bunch of bucks to just audition with the group so that he could get the trio signed. At the last minute they would replace me, he said, but this would insure his trio getting signed with Tommy for the tour. So I agreed, knowing that I would pull out.

The next afternoon I was at the Algiers Hotel. I met the three guys and found them to be really good, honest, hard-working musicians. Leon Bagwell, bass; Eddie Edwards, rhythm guitar; and Scotty Turnbull on electric guitar. I had no idea that these three hillbillies would change the course of my career and my life.

Leon Bagwell was a slap bass player. A good-looking Texan in the mold of Rock Hudson, he spoke with the most countrified drawl

I had ever heard. I knew Leon was green to the business, hailing from Loop, Texas, and having been a dirt farmer all of his 19 or 20 years. Leon was the tall, silent type, but boy, could he slap the shit out of that old upright bass!

Eddie Edwards was from San Saba, Texas, famous for it's shell pecans. Eddie was the comedian of the group. He was also a great rhythm guitar player, but it took me the longest time to get used to his snuff spitting. Eddie was featured on songs like *Who Wears Short Shorts*. Audiences loved his antics.

Scotty Turnbull, from Lachine, Quebec, Canada, was a misture of country and rock and roll. He was one hell of a picker and songwriter, and Tommy recorded a bunch of his soungs. The trio had met at Texas Tech and formed a group. (That's where their name, the Texas Raiders, came from.)

We all sat down to our instruments, and one of the guys started pickin' and grinnin' and I fell in playing with them. I didn't know this tune from Adam. I just played. They did a standard ending and that was that. Unknown to us, Tommy and his manager, Ted Wick, were standing in the hallway and listening just outside the open door. When we finished *Bucket*, Tommy and Ted walked in and greeted us with, "Well, you found the right drummer, let's go on the road!"

Ted Wick was a lovable, pudgy, round-faced man with a broad smile, obviously wise to the world. I was about 27 at the time and Ted took me aside and said, "I can see that you really know what you're doing and I need an experienced man as road manager for this crew. How about drumming and being the road manager and I'll start you out at three hundred a week?" I said, "Let me think about it." Ted quipped "Don't think about it too long, you're leaving next week!" We spent the rest of the afternoon running over tunes, and it seemed like I did everything right. Tommy was impressed, the kids were impressed, and in no time we had a mutual admiration society going.

I spent the next few days with Tommy and the group and really fell in love with everything they were doing. I knew that going to New York and doing the Gary Moore Show and the Perry Como Show wasn't the worst thing that could happen. Here I was, the drummer in a name group– the chance of a lifetime for a showoff like me. This would also be an opportunity for my folks to finally see me perform and maybe understand that there might be a future for me in this crazy business.

The next weeks were my initiation into the really big time. Fans screaming, ripping at our clothing, signing autographs, leaping into limos. Working state fairs with people like Gabby Hayes and Johnny Cash, Sky King and Penny. This was it. Walking the midways and filling up on sweet com on the cob. Being treated with more respect than I had ever known.

Tommy seemed unaffected by all of this publicity, except when we were about to board an airplane. He would suddenly disappear. They would have to hold up the plane while I went searching. I'd always find him at the magazine stand reading his movie magazines. He was in every one of them. I even started seeing my puss in one now and then.

The guys in the band were just wonderful. They taught me more about the true "feel" of country music than I could have ever learned in a school. I was tuned in to every hit of the day and we were doing a lot of them onstage.

Whenever possible we would visit Leon's and Eddie's hometowns. The red carpet would be rolled out for the hometown kids who made it big. We were quite the celebrities in Texas and Canada, and the parents of these kids treated me like a son. More than that, we had all become like brothers, which posed some challenges along the way.

I'll never forget when we worked the Starlite Room of the Waldorf Hotel in New York City with the Count Basie Band. It was an incredible experience. Count's drummer, Sonny Payne, had gotten sick and, naturally, yours truly got to play the gig. I knew most of the charts, and now there I was, kicking my favorite Big Band. It was every drummer's dream in those days.

Count Basie, the gentleman of the keyboard, even offered me the job of a lifetime. "I'll make you the most famous white drummer in the world!" I was flabbergasted. What an opportunity! But I explained that Tommy's job was my job and I couldn't think of leaving the group. We had worked so hard, and these guys were brothers to me. Count even offered me the job as road manager along with the drum chair if I reconsidered, but there was no reconsidering.

It was many years later that I was walking through the hallway of United Studios in Hollywood and heard that unmistakable sound from Studio A. I popped my head into the booth and Count was at the console listening to a playback After the tape stopped and everyone agreed that was the take, I quietly walked up to him and reintroduced myself. I said, "Count, I don't know if you remember me or not, but" He interrupted me, "Hal Blaine, as much drums as you play, you think I'm gonna forget you?"

Everything was going wonderfully with the Tommy Sands show. I was getting some great studio experience with Tommy doing his records. I was meeting all of the producers at Capitol Records and I was working in Tommy's films doing bit parts, standing in for Tommy and later working with many notables. We were working at the Sands Hotel where we recorded *Sands at the Sands*, my first Big Band show album. Unfortunately, it was also the start of the finish for our group, The Raiders, now called The Sharks, a name we adopted after playing Hawaii a number of times for the great promoter Tom Moffatt. The Sharks were coming to a close because Tommy was going to start playing the big rooms only. Big orchestras couldn't really use country pickers.

Then came the night we had been waiting for. We had played all of the top TV shows out of New York – Perry Como, Gary Moore, Ed Sullivan and the like. We were playing all of the major nightclubs around the country, and in between we were flying in and out of Hollywood recording at Capitol Records.

The Coconut Grove was the big one, though. We had been building to this event for three years. L.A., the toughest town for any entertainer. The houselights dimmed. Jeff Lewis threw the timpanist his cue to start the thunderous roll. The curtain came up over the announcer's offstage introduction, and the goosebumps started, reminding me of my front row center Saturdays, back in the State Theater. But this was L.A., now my hometown too.

It was such an emotional experience. This was it as far as I was concerned. If I never did another thing in the business, I knew I had made it. All of the Tommy Sand fans were there along with Tommy's friends, mostly celebrities themselves. These were the new generation of Hollywoodites. Tommy Sands was a top draw.

And there she was – sitting ringside. I had only seen her pictures in fan magazines with her dad. But here, in person, was Nancy with the laughing face. Even from my drum seat I could see the look in her eyes. I guess she was more or less seeing the image of her dad up there, the handsome young crooner in the classy tuxedo. I think I was more excited than Tommy.

Well, the show was a knockout. After the applause died down we were back in the dressing room welcoming the continuous stream of Hollywood well-wishers, acquaintances and friends. Each time the door opened and the *maitre'd* announced another name we would look at each other in shock and excitement. And then the big one for all of us – Nancy Sinatra.

Tommy was about 19 then and Nancy was about 17. After their first meeting they were constantly together. From the first date it was a love affair. Nancy insisted on being on the road with us, and we all fell in love with her. She was everybody's friend, kid sister, and mentor. She had kind words for everyone and wasn't at all the spoiled Hollywood brat some had thought. Nancy had gone to public schools and was surprisingly normal.

Nancy Sinatra Sr. turned out to be the exact same way. Nancy's mother was an Italian mother, the counterpart of a Jewish mother. There was always food on the table, and I was constantly amazed to find Nancy Sr. making drapes for the living room or sewing someone's torn clothing. Her opening line was always something like, "Com'on. You must be hungry," just like my mom.

Tommy's mother Grace and "Big Nancy," (as we all affectionately called her) consented to Nancy coming out on the road with us on one condition: either or both of them would come along and chaperone the lovebirds. I remember a wonderful trip to Vancouver, British Columbia, when we all drove together and Tommy and Nancy were just inseparable. Grace would say, "Now look you kids, no hanky panky!" and we would laugh for hours. There was no hanky-panky. We all had separate rooms and I know how tough it was for them. Watching those kids was a show in itself, especially when they were saying goodnight and fighting to keep their hands off each other.

The following weeks were great fun for me because I got to meet so many of the fans and celebrities associated with the Sinatra clan. I met Frank and Frankie and all of the Sinatra relatives – and I was made to feel right at home.

Tommy and Nancy's engagement party was a blowout affair. Every star I had ever heard of was there. Tommy and Nancy were married not too long after that. They were the happiest couple around. They lived in a white apartment that Auntie Tina decorated, and it was gorgeous. Frank often called the kids when we were performing, and he always said, "Blainey, pick up the check and sign my name!" The kids lived a fairy tale life, often going to Dad's house in Palm Springs, and on special occasions I was lucky enough to be invited along.

The marriage didn't last too long, though. In a short time it seemed like the perfect marriage wasn't that perfect after all. Maybe these kids were just too young. No one knows the reason for sure, but they did eventually break up, and Tommy more or less quit the business. Rumors had it that Frank Sinatra put out the word that Sands was not to work anywhere, but insiders knew it was total hogwash.

Tommy called me just prior to his move to Hawaii and told me he didn't really want to work anymore. He wanted to find himself and get back on the right track. He just had to get away, and what better place than Hawaii with his old friend Tom Moffatt.

Tom took care of Tommy for a long time. In those days he was the top disc jockey on KPOI. My feelings were that this teenager had gotten too much too soon and just couldn't handle it. He wasn't prepared.

Tommy had been retired for some time and was attending college when Tom Moffatt talked him into putting together an act for the Outrigger Hotel. Tommy did really well there. One year when I came over I decided to surprise him. While he was doing his act, I snuck backstage and got on the drums. Tommy finished his speech to the audience and away we went doing the Hawaiian favorite, *Ain't No Big Ting Bruddah*. In a matter of seconds Tommy turned and somehow just knew it was me. We had a wonderful reunion.

6

Patti Page and the Movies

When Tommy Sands left for Hawaii I wasn't sure what band I'd play with next. I jobbed around with the wonderful Vido Musso Band, backing Vido on various casuals (we referred to them as "casualties"). We worked places like the Slate Brothers in Hollywood and backed Don Rickles. (I used to laugh so hard that Don would look at me and quip, "Get a table, will ya, Hal") I also traveled with Vido to San Francisco to back Frances Faye, a very hip entertainer in those days.

Another great piece of basic training transpired with Vido and Frances at the infamous Facks Number 2 Nitery. Unbeknownst to me at the time, Frances had a way of throwing curves at drummers – as part of her act. She would have the drummer set up very close to her, and in the middle of whatever tempo we'd be playing she'd go off into some other tempo leaving the drummer with egg on his face.

We rehearsed all sorts of tunes at her palatial mansion in the Hollywood Hills, but when it came to opening night I had to forget all of her arrangements. She immediately did her thing, going off into these other tempos, but I was on my toes and immediately noticed that every time she went into another tempo her right foot went to the sustain pedal on the piano. I was now ready for anything!

After we finished the first show, Frances called me into the dressing room. "Okay pal, how do you do it? No drummer has ever done it before!" I started to laugh and asked her what she was talking about. "You know what I'm talking about!" she said, and started a rap about my ESP. She did a radio talk show the next day and talked practically the whole time about her drummer, the clairvoyant!

During the dance sets I was the singer in the band. One night, a gentleman and lady asked me to sit down and have a drink. I explained that I wasn't drinking because I was on medication for a sore throat. (That always works and no one is ever offended.) I ordered a tall orange juice. This guy told me how much he liked my singing. Something about his voice had a familiar ring. I introduced myself and he said, "This is Kathy and I'm Bing." Well, the shakes took over and I was beside myself. This was my introduction to the famous Crosbys.

A few years later I recorded with Bing, doing his only rock record, The Beatles' *Hey Jude* with a great Jimmie Haskell arrangement. Bing even saw to it that we went overtime, a trick he used to do all the time. He would finish a take that would be great, look at the clock and see that there were only a couple of minutes left on the session. Then he'd rap a minute to the producer and say, "Let's do one more just in case it might be better." We'd start the take and that would run the clock a few minutes into overtime. Then Bing would stop and say, "Well, let's forget it, I think the last one was the one." We all applauded.

When I finished the San Francisco gig and came back to L.A., I got a call from the great composer/arranger Jack Elliot. I had never met the man, but evidently he had heard of me or seen me, and he asked if I was available for Vegas to do a month at the Desert Inn. And how! I was to take Bobby Rosengarden's place with the Patti Page show, and I was thrilled. Bobby had gone back to New York and was making quite a name for himself in the Big Apple. Patti's manager Jack Rael was a sweetheart with a great broad smile; I think he liked my Jewish humor, and we traveled around the country for the next three years.

Patti was a gal from Oklahoma, one of 11 siblings. She was a real country girl, but Hollywood and her singing success forced her to grow up in a hurry. We rehearsed at her beautiful Canon Drive home in Beverly Hills for a few days, and this was my introduction to some of the nicest people in the business. Patti and her husband at the time, Charles O'Curran, were completely down-to-earth people; no Hollywood bullshit. Charlie was a choreographer at Paramount for years, and had the respect of the entire industry. He also had a great sense of humor.

His sense of staging was impeccable. Charlie hid an autoharp inside the piano so that at one point in the show when the lights came down dramatically, Patti walked to the open piano and ran her fingers over the concealed auto harp as if she were strumming the regular piano strings; she sang *Danny Boy*. Of course, the chords were all perfect coming from the autoharp, but the audience thought that she was doing it with the piano strings. You could almost see the teardrops falling as everyone imagined they were hearing an angel. What a show stopper!

During that Desert Inn job in Vegas I met the woman who I consider to be my first real wife. Lydia was a beautiful 18-year-old blonde from New Orleans. I was now about 32, but the age difference didn't seem to mean a thing to either of us. I had been dating another blonde dancer at the Inn who had gone to Reno with a dance troupe. During her stay at the Golden Hotel, there was a fire and she perished. I was devastated.

Lydia was a very dear friend of this dancer/ice skater, and we had been casually introduced in Vegas. After the dancer's death, Lydia contacted me to find out what happened. We fell in love and married soon after. We adopted two wonderful kids, purchased a Hollywood Hills home and life was sweet.

After eight years, though, Lydia decided that there was more to life than living with a workaholic musician and she decided on a divorce. One year later, while living in Long Beach, California, she took her own life. I immediately picked up our children, Michelle and David, and brought them home.

During the years that I worked with Patti I usually came back to Hollywood between engagements, and it was during these times that I became friendly with H. B. Barnum. H. B. was an arranger/composer who always had something on the fire. If it wasn't a nightclub, it was a private party at a ballroom, or a gig at an air base, or maybe just a backyard barbecue. He started using me in the studios doing demos and the like, and then moved me up to full-fledged studio drummer. I got to work with Sam Cooke and various artists of the day, and he gave me great opportunities to develop my studio techniques. It was wonderful hearing myself on playbacks and trying new things on different takes. Before long, I began to discover what sounded best. By trial and error I got the studio experience I needed to make it into the front ranks of session players.

43

I was working with the Diamonds when I first met Earl Palmer. Earl was the King of the Mountain, and I learned more from him than I could have learned from a music library. Earl had been Fats Domino's drummer and he had that New Orleans style down pat. He was doing most of the major rock dates in town and after a while he started tossing my name around and recommending me for gigs that he couldn't make. Before long, I was working with the best and meeting most of the famous musicians in L.A. It was on Earl's recommendation that I started with the Tijuana Brass. That led to my first Record of the Year, *A Taste of Honey*. As important as knowing the musicians was getting to know the popular contractors of the day, the guys that did all of the hiring. They were the real bosses– they could make you or break you, and often did both.

I had now begun to learn many of the lessons that relate to success in the music business. And I saw it many times – there are no losers in any business, just winners that give up too soon. This business is like any other. You must know your trade. You must study all aspects and be ready when your time comes. One of the worst things that can happen to people in any business is taking a major job when you're not ready for it, especially in the record business where time is money. Anyone can make a mistake, but when you make the same mistake repeatedly, the contractors remember your name and there go your calls. Learn your instrument, study your reading and listen to everything you can. Learn every conceivable style of music, because you never know what they're going to throw at you. And then make up some of your own – the stuff you really feel.

It was during one of my layoffs with Patti that Charles O'Curran called and asked me to come to a meeting at Paramount. I entered the music stage and was ushered into a small room off the main studio. Sitting in the room were several Paramount executives. The only faces I recognized were Charles and Phil Kahgan, the musical contractor at Paramount Pictures for 50 years. He was the giant of giants among contractors.

A few years before, on Tommy Sands' *Love in a Goldfish Bowl* film, it had taken a lot of begging by Jimmie Haskell to convince Kahgan that I was in fact a drummer, as opposed to being an actor. After Jimmie convinced Kahgan, he reluctantly hired me and then, fortunately, continued to hire me for my entire career.

Charlie waved to me and pointed to a seat. I sat down and the speech began. "We're going to be doing a new film with Hal Wallis directing (pointing to Mr. Wallis seated front and center,) and I want the best of the best on this picture. It's a very important picture and it might mean a lot of extra hours and a lot of extra work on your parts, but we want this picture to be the best, in the old tradition of Paramount. It's a young people's musical set in Hawaii, and I want you to meet the star." And with that the star entered. It was Elvis Presley in the flesh.

Working on an Elvis movie like *Blue Hawaii* was a great learning experience for many of us in Hollywood. Rock and roll had been infiltrating the movie scene slowly but surely. Producers started using small rock segments as source music in order to keep their films up to date. After all, rock and roll was already a dominant part of the American radio scene.

When I arrived at the Music Stage at 20th Century-Fox, my drums were set up near the back with one large microphone in front of the bass drum. Obviously these recording engineers hadn't been keeping up with the multi-microphone techniques becoming popular in the rock-oriented Hollywood recording studios. While this barn-like studio had hosted countless sessions with the masters of music, things were changing quickly in recording, and the film studios were not keeping up with the times. We started playing the chart, and before long the producer of the film came out, complaining to the arranger that the music didn't sound like what he had been hearing on the radio. My drums sounded like they were a mile away. The producer then asked me why they sounded so distant and I explained what we had been doing in Hollywood with multi-miking and baffling off the drums for isolation, and so on. He called a break and asked the engineers to come down from the third floor sound booth and to do what I thought was best.

Well, I told them how in Hollywood we put a mic in front of the bass drum and one on the snare, one on the hi-hat and one or two overhead. The engineers threw up their hands in disgust and told me I was nuts. "I'm only telling you what's going on at the rock studios in Hollywood," I said, as the contractor gave me a dirty look. I was starting to think that I would probably never get another call from 20th. All of the band was sitting around watching me dig my own grave. I was the new kid on this block, and here I was telling the biggies what I thought they should do. The engineers screamed that they didn't have enough lines or inputs to mike a set of drums that way. Drums were always in the background, back in those days of 4-track and less.

Nonetheless, some electrical people were called in, a few jerryrigged connections were made, and some baffles were put in place.

We cut the tracks again, and everyone agreed they were perfect. After all was said and done, I became something of a hero there and got called back for many soundtracks.

Hal's

Scrapbook

Mom and Dad in their liquor store in Santa Monica during the early Sixties

Nineteen and just out of the army, I break in my first set of Slingerlands with The Novelteers at Tommy's Ranch House in Great Falls, Montana

One side of the Stan Moore Trio. Left to right, Stan, me and Keith Curtiss in 1949.

Another side of The Trio, a.k.a. The Novelteers. We were a "funny hat band."

The Hal Blaine Quartet, featuring Vicki Young, at the Magic Carpet in San Bernardino, California, in 1952

(photo: Al Newman)

I played "stand-up" drums in 1953 with my band, The Guys & Dolls, at the Falcon Room of the Colorado Springs Hotel. To my roght, Bunky Jones, Nancy Malcomb, and Susan Evans.

The first producer I ever worked with was Bill Bellman
(right) in 1954. He was also San Bernardino's top DJ on KRNO,
and at least as crazy as I was. (photo: Rhea Fossum)

At the Diplomat Hotel in Hollywood, Florida, in 1961
with Patti Page. Rocky Cole conducted her fine band.

Playing in Tommy Sands' band, in 1957, was my introduction to rock and roll. Left to right: Tommy, me, Eddie Edwards, Leon Bagwell, and Scott Turner

Tommy is the one with the hands. (Photo: Lipp Studio)

Backing up Jan & Dean in concert at the Hollywood Bowl.
(photo: Jasper Dailey)

Jan Berry was the daredevil. (Larry Knechtel on right)

Dean Torrence was the pussycat.

The Wrecking Crew celebrates another knockout session with Phil Spector.

Working on a Beach Boys session at Western Studio Three with Ray Pohlman (center) and Lyle Ritz (right)

(photo: Jasper Dailey)

Lead Beach Boy Brian Wilson frequently asked our opinions on his arrangements. This was about 1964 in Western's Studio Three.

The Wrecking Crew at work in Gold Star Studios, circe 1963. Clockwise from front left: Al Delory, Carol Kaye, Tommy Tedesco, (unidentified), Roy Caton, Jay Migliori, Hal Blaine, Steve Douglas, (unidentified), Ray Pohlman.

Guitar Ace Tommy Tedesco was a familiar sight in the studio, as was upright bassist Chuck Berghoffer. *(photo: Jasper Dailey)*

Wrecking Crewmen Billy Strange (top) Don Randi (bottom) and I share an astounded reaction. *(photo: Jasper Dailey)*

Prior to The Wrecking Crew, Red Callender was the West Coast Studio bassist who played rock as well as jazz.

The Chicken Sax Man, Steve Douglas, laid down solos for everybody from Duane Eddy to The Beach Boys.

Glen Campbell brought outrageous country-inspired guitar solos to The Wrecking Crew— & a strong-willed desire to break out on his own.

Carol Kaye was not only the sweetheart of The Wrecking Crew, but was solid as a rock on electric bass.

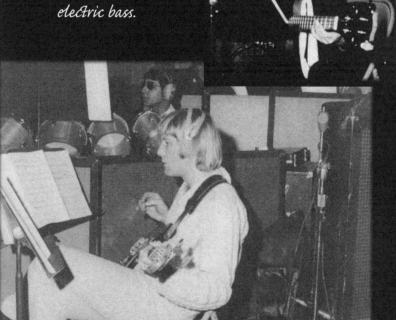

We called Larry Knechtel Prince Valiant, but never doubted his abilities on bass or grand piano. He played the classic piano intro on "Bridge Over Troubled Water." (photo: Jasper Dailey)

Red- hot producer Snuff Garrett with Lou Morell (left) and Tommy Tedesco (right.)

Te all-time top studio oboist on the West Coast has to be Gene Cipriano.

Herb Alpert (left) and Julius Wechter (later with The Baja Marimba Band) at Sunset Sound Recorders

Billy Strange and Nancy Sinatra set the stage to record "These Boots Are Made for Walkin."

The Chairman of the Board had infinite class, and we studio cats were always on our best behavior when he was around.

Dean Martin between takes on "Everybody Loves Somebody."
Guitarist Glen Campbell is on the right.

Discussing an arrangement with Sammy Davis, Jr. (left), Ray
Pohlman and producer Jimmy Bowen on my right.
(photo: Jasper Dailey)

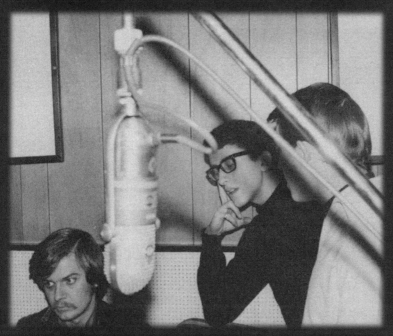

Left to right: A young Leon Russell works with Gary Lewis and his vocal coach Ron Hicklin on "This Diamond Ring."

"If You Can't Beat 'Em, Join 'Em" was the name of this mid-Sixties Gerry Mulligan album. Left to right; Gerry, me, Jimmy Bond, and Pete Jolly. (photo: Fred Seligo)

Here they come.... again!

Another round of Gold Records from Warner Brothers/Reprise big wigs. Left to right: Moe Austin, me, Jimmy Bowen, and Joe Smith. The records (left to right): "These Boots Are Made For Walkin", "My Love," and "Strangers In The Night."

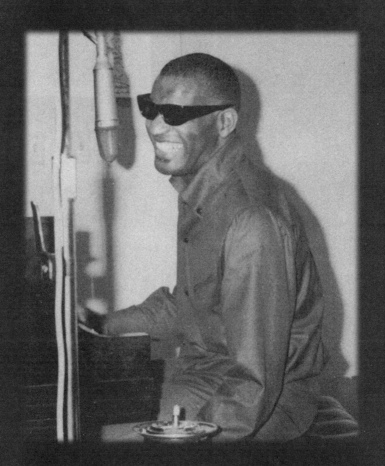

The genius of Ray Charles at his RPM Studio in Inglewood, California in the mid-Sixties.

Working with the great pianist Buddy Greco on "The More I See You." Left to right: Jimmy Bowen, Jimmy Webb, Buddy, and me.
(photo: Jasper Dailey)

My first set of
electronic drums. If you
can't beat 'em, turn up
the volume.
(photo: Richard Schumacher)

In L.A. you gotta
have a car.

*Mamas Michelle Phillips and Cass Elliot take the stage
with their drummer boy (me).* (photo: Jasper Dailey)

Papa Denny Doherty discovers a new microphone technique.

Papa John Phillips wrote the tunes and played the guitar.

Super producer Lou Adler began to look more and more like one of his Mamas and Papas as time went on.

Gravelly-voiced Barry McGuire became a one-hit wonder after we cut his "Eve of Destruction."

Working with the phenomenal songwriter Jimmy Webb (left) at about the time of "MacArthur Park." (Photo: Jasper Dailey)

Producer Bones Howe (right) and I celebrate at the Grammy Awards for winning Record Of The YEar, with The Fifth Dimension for "Aquarius/Let The Sun Shine."
(Photo: Jasper Dailey)

Mike Deasy, a latter day Wrecking Crewman, was our mystical guru of guitar sounds when psychedelia entered the studios.

Adding a little extra percussion to Mel Taylor's
(The Ventures) drumming.   *(photo: Jasper Dailey)*

John Denver's traveling road show in the mid-Seventies included an
up and coming comic named Jay Leno (far right, just below me.)

On the road with Duane Eddy during his 1984 revival tour.

c. 1958 at New York's Waldorf-Astoria with Joe Williams on my right, Count Basie on my left. Nearly 40 years later, my daughter Michelle went to the Waldorf on my behalf to accept one of my highest honors, induction into the Rock Hall of Fame.

The monster drum setup that set a new standard
for rock studio drummers.

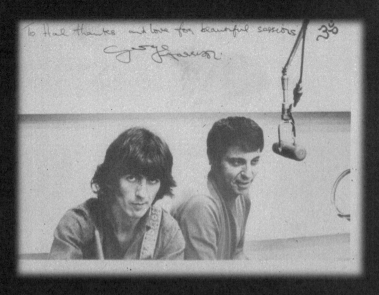

To Hal thanks and love for beautiful sessions ॐ

George Harrison

George Harrison like the sound of my concert toms so
much , he bought an identical set for Ringo.

*August 24, 2002: Delivering a lecture from behind the famous kit,
as part of the NAMM oral history program.*

The drums on display at the 2008 NAMM show.

7

Phil Spector & The Wrecking Crew

The sessions with Phil Spector at the helm were truly amazing; the results will live forever. There was a familiar magic whenever we walked into Gold Star Studios. Phil had the magic wand and sprinkled fairy dust on us all. The Wrecking Crew, as we began calling our group of regular session players, was the envy of the recording industry.

There were always little signs hanging around the studio, proclaiming things like "Phil the King." Phil himself would stick goofy signs on us like, "Hi! I'm Betty Boop!" or "I'm W. C. Fields' mother-in-law!" It was pure comedy from the moment we entered the studio. Every member of The Wrecking Crew was lavished with crazy gifts like a pair of garters or a box of rubbers, always beautifully gift wrapped. Phil once handed me a present, rather heavy, and as all the guys stood by watching with anticipation, I opened the neatly wrapped gift– it was a perfectly sculptured, red and white striped peppermint candy penis. Phil's sessions maintained a state of barely controlled chaos.

He would be jumping all over the booth, conducting the engineer, Larry Levine, and bumping into friends and musicians strewn around the control room. We were having such a ball, and we knew that we were making history. Phil's "Wall of Sound" was the hottest thing in music all over the world.

Phil had a way of holding me back while the band rehearsed. I felt like a racehorse who wants to run as soon as the gate opens, and Phil, the jockey, would rein me in until we were coming around the clubhouse turn, heading for the final stretch. When the right take materialized, he would start his incredible gyrations in the booth, running from one side of the glass to the other, looking at key people during crucial moments like Leonard Bernstein conducting the New York Philharmonic.

He would conduct with one hand asking for loudness, while the other hand was directed at another section calling for quiet. Then he would give me that magical look that meant only one thing – Go! And we would both go crazy, me doing fills that were total lunacy. I would do eighth-note and 16th-note fills during a shuffle, and vice versa.

One particular lick that I came up with during these bursts of madness stuck and became a regular Spector trademark: quarter-note triplets played against what the band was doing. The record was never done until Phil cued me to do triplets. (My friend Max Weinberg, Bruce Springsteen's drummer, once told me that he and Bruce were raised on Phil Spector records and that Bruce often looks at Max during sessions and shouts "Hal Blaine!" meaning those fills.)

The recording dates were always clearly marked "Closed Session," but anyone who poked his head in was told to come in, sit down, or go grab an instrument and play. It was a well-known secret that the "Closed Session" sign was more like a welcome sign. Every producer in town "Just happened" to be passing Gold Star and wanted to say hi to Phil. Actually, every producer and artist wanted to have the magic touch them, so there were usually more people in the booth than in the studio.

Some of the artists who came by were out of work, and Phil would often "throw a bone" to the people who needed a helping hand. For instance, Sonny Bono was working for a record distribution company at the time, and he had just started dating Cher, who was singing backgrounds now and then. Sometimes Sonny would play one of my cowbells or shake my shakers during a take, and Phil would put him on contract and let him make a few bucks. Frank Capp, Gene Estes, Gary Coleman, Terry Gibbs, and I or the other regular percussionists would bring crates of percussion toys to these dates and it got to the point where as many as eight or ten people would be playing castanets, shakers, jingle bells, bongos, congas, puili sticks, slap-sticks, tambourines and any other gadget they could find in the percussion crates.

The "Wall of Sound" was literally that. Remember, these were the early days of recording, and echo was about the only special effect that studios had. But our engineer, Larry Levine, had some tricks, and every time he came up with a new one Phil would beam and want to use it on the record.

We would rehearse for hours and hours, and no one could even go to the toilet for fear of moving a mic. Finally, after endless run-throughs, Phil would call a "ten" and scream, "Don't touch the mics!" And no one did.

I clearly remember how carefully we would all get up, twisting our bodies and moving delicately. Phil had positioned the rnics himself, and the placement was sacred. like ballet dancers, we would step around the mics and over the cords strewn all over Studio A. The heat was incredible. There was no real air conditioning in those days before they remodeled the studio. We used to say that the flies buzzing around the Gold Star were getting as large and as famous as us musicians.

Phil Spector is the only producer I've ever known who always had an extra 2-track recorder running constantly from the beginning of every session. Everything said or played went on tape, and it was quite a trick. Musicians often walk into the studio cold and start warming up in their own way before the tracking begins. They come up with strange riffs, and when asked what they've played they never remember. Not so at Phil's sessions. He would ask, play back the lick, and say, "Remember that. I want it on the front of the bridge." Phil would pick out the nuggets he wanted and by playing them back, make them history. (So many musicians play incredible warm-ups and never even know it.)

Phil's "Wall of Sound" was not only making a name for itself, it was making a name for all of us involved. Although we often had more than a dozen musicians on any given session, there were several rhythm players who always seemed to be on the hits. I was fortunate to be a part of one section who worked together constantly. The band typically consisted of Carol Kaye and Ray Pohlman on Fender basses; Lyle Ritz and Jimmy Bond on upright basses; Tommy Tedesco, Barney Kessel, Howard Roberts, Glen Campbell and Bill Pittman on guitars; Don Randi, Leon Russell, Larry Knechtel, Michael Melvoin and Al Delory on pianos. There was always a host of percussionists, and at various times different piano players, guitarists, drummers and horn men. Jack Nitzsche usually did the chord charts, and I was usually on drums. I missed a few of the monster hits, like the Righteous Brothers' *You've Lost That Lovin' Feeling,"* which was given that lovin' touch by Earl Palmer. Steve Douglas was usually on sax along with Nino

Tempo (April Stevens and Nino had the big hit *Deep Purple*,) Jay Migliori and Roy Caton on trumpet along with Ollie Mitchell and Tony Terran. Virgil Evans, Lou Blackburn and other horn men substituted from time to time.

We came along behind the well-schooled demigod session players of Hollywood. These were the studio musicians who were honored and revered. They were the veterans, well-trained in the pop and classical fields, who had worked with all the popular bands from the radio and TV shows of the '40s and '50s. These were the troops who could, and literally did, read fly shit off the chart if it happened to be there. Their abilities were incredible.

Before rock and roll came along and transformed the business, the pop music scene had been great in its own way. The musicianship was superb, and the masses enjoyed the music they grew up with during the war years. There was a soft, light sound that made you miss your brother, your husband, your lover. Music could make you feel patriotic, urge you to send packages to the boys overseas and volunteer to work in hospitals to get the awful mess over with. The film scene was the same – you missed your loved ones and the scores tugged at your heart. Everyone had someone "over there," and we were bombarded with patriotism 24 hours a day. The general public had not yet experienced the new music that was coming down the road – the rock road and the country road. It was down and dirty, rebellious, anarchistic and sexually free. It was the music of a generation of kids brought up on ration coupons and the smell of Korea. Now it was our turn to write and sing what we felt.

Our time had come and we were taking the music world by storm. We were known as a group who cared about making music, not just taking the money and running to the Cadillac agency. We had a special "feel," a key word in understanding this new sound. We felt the song, listened to the lyric. We cared for the music, the artist, the writer. This was something new in the Hollywood music business. It's not that the older, well-respected musicians didn't care, but when we worked with many of the regulars, it seemed more like a job to them. It seemed like they wanted to get the session over with and get off to the golf course.

As for our nickname, The Wrecking Crew, it came about because that was the impression we gave the older musicians. The established studio musicians always wore their blue blazers and neckties and always cleaned their ashtrays after a date. We were the new guys, and we dressed as we lived – in Levi's and T-shirts. We were informal and spontaneous, and a lot of the old hands thought we were wrecking the music industry.

It didn't take long for the word to get around that a new breed of musicians was making the hits. We were new in town, and it seemed like everything we touched turned to gold. Our sudden success was phenomenal. We were booked weeks and weeks in advance, sometimes months ahead. Producers coming in from New York would demand the West Coast guys who were making the new hits. They wanted the same guys, the same studios (usually Gold Star, Western, United and Sound Recorders) and the same hitmaking engineers, such as Bones Howe, Stan Ross, Larry Levine, Chuck Britz, Eddie Brackett and Lee Hershberg.

Producers knew that our involvement with a production was different, too. Nine times out of ten the arranger would say, "I don't like what I've written," or the producer would say, "I'm not really satisfied with this score." They would tell us to use the charts as a guide, and that's all. We were encouraged to go for it, to go beyond what had been written. We had the opportunity to create, to be a team of arrangers – 20 players who would really listen to each other and maybe say, "Hey, Tommy's into something here," or "Don's really stretching it. I'm going to try something new." I might get into a new groove with Carol on bass, or play off Earl's drumming, and it would start a chain reaction. The collaboration and continually surprising magic became second nature to all of us.

The huge diversity of backgrounds our musicians had may have been responsible for this new spirit and sound. I'd guess that 90 percent of our group had some jazz or academic background. We had studied, done shows and were well-trained. We had enough confidence to hang loose, and we felt free to experiment. The country musicians who joined us weren't exactly academics, though they added important new elements to our chemistry. The jazzers could keep rock solid time, and guys like Glen Campbell, Billy Strange and James Burton would bring wild, off-the-wall solos that had never been heard before. Putting all of this on a rock and roll record was totally fresh.

You should understand that most of us Easterners thought of country musicians as hillbillies. They were unpolished, unschooled musicians who played a style of music very different from the Big Band, Swing Era styles that had dominated Hollywood until we all converged simultaneously on the scene in the late '50s.

Glen Campbell was especially interesting – a real live hillbilly from Delight, Arkansas, who took Hollywood by storm. He couldn't read a note of music, but the record-buying public was eating him up. He had incorporated country-style electric guitar into rock music, and his solos injected an uninhibited, savage, raw feeling into the records. He played a big part in transforming the pop and rock scene.

Leon Russell was another hillbilly-type from Tulsa, Oklahoma. When I first met him, he was a skinny, short-haired kid who had suffered the ravages of polio as a child. He limped noticeably in those early years, but when he sat down at the piano, he turned the record business upside down. Every producer wanted Leon Russell, also known early on as Russell Bridges. Like Glen, Leon brought savage solos to our sessions and added a key element to our hit record formula.

Billy Strange came out of the backwoods too: a cowboy who could make a guitar talk. Billy was a very underrated player whose roots were strictly country, but with a jazz touch thrown in. He was conductor for Tennessee Ernie Ford's TV show out of San Francisco. Billy was never seen without his cowboy boots. He was a hulk of a guy, well over six feet tall, and awesome with those boots on. He had a great knowledge and intuition for arranging and was a noted songwriter. Billy was one of the exceptions to the rule that all country musicians are self-taught. He could read well and had a broad knowledge of the music business. He also had a strong background in studio recording from years of working at Capitol with many of the famous artists of the day. Billy was instrumental in directing us newcomers to the complexity of studio life.

Tommy Tedesco, a legendary musician, was another founding father of our new sound. Tommy came from a different direction. He was a well-trained guitarist from Buffalo and a real New Yorker. Tommy was one of those bird dogs who helped us in times of need. When an arranger pulled out one of those incredible scores and laid a part in front of us that was literally blackened with notes, Tommy would be the first to lean over and calmly decipher the tough passages. He saved many a session that would have ended in disaster, and saved many of us from ulcers. Tommy and I became very close in those days, and I mean close. We often worked 12 to 14 hours a day, side by side, and then laid down next to our instruments at 4 a.m. to catch a little rest before an 8 a.m. session.

Lyle Ritz, an upright bass player (at a time when the electric Fender bass was taking over the recording scene), was another mainstay of The Wrecking Crew. Very mild mannered, Lyle was a funny, funny man who had a smile for everyone. He had fallen into the position of having to play his upright in unison with a Fender because the engineers and producers found that the two basses played together created a much "fatter" sound, providing the perfect bottom for records. This was during the 2- and 4-track days, before overdubbing made it possible for one player to get that kind of fat sound.

Carol Kaye was the lone female musician in the Crew. Carol is truly a musician's musician and has received much praise. Originally an incredible jazz guitarist, Carol (Kahalavich) picked up a Fender bass one day and the rest is history. She was a killer bass player who never let you down and never got in your way. We made such solid music together – I often thought that this was the woman I should have married.

Don Randi: pianist extraordinaire, jazz aficionado, New Yorker to the nth degree, also known as "Schwartzy." He was a classically trained pianist and another key ingredient in our recipe for the hit sound. My first meeting with Don was a wild and funny date–a Spector session. We worked the night away, and during the breaks we talked and became friendly. We were just a couple of Jew boys from the East Coast trying to make it in Hollywood. We were easy and cordial in our "See ya laters," and the next morning I hopped a plane for Manny Skar's Sahara Inn in Chicago. I was traveling with the Patti Page Show and after a quick band rehearsal, we opened on a Saturday night. After the show, I walked downstairs to the lounge and heard this incredible trio blowing their brains out on stage. I was yanked in by the music and nearly fell over in surprise. There was Don Randi with his group. What a great treat and quick reunion, and what a ball we had that week.

After The Wrecking Crew made its mark on the music scene, Phil Spector went off to do his own thing. No one really knew what he was up to until we realized that some of the big Beatles hits were his productions. I hadn't seen him for some time, and then I got a call from Donna, his Girl Friday, asking me to do some dates. The old band was reassembled for some special sessions for Leonard Cohen at Gold Star and at Whitney Studios in Glendale. They were incredible dates. There was one major change, though – we had the Kessel brothers (Barney's sons.) Phil was now hiring the second generation of Hollywood musicians. Once again, everyone in town dropped by to hang out. Here was Cher, Bob Dylan with his wife, and Allen Ginsberg, all singing backgrounds for Leonard Cohen. They couldn't quite get the hang of coming in at the right places, so Phil asked me to conduct the chorus on overdubs. Jeez, it was fun to be working with the master again.

But it was all leading up to the big one: the John Lennon project. Jim Keltner called and asked if I would work double drums with him for Phil's sessions with Lennon. This was the West Coast album that John did before going to New York for his last work. Of course I said that I'd be thrilled to be there.

Once again a new Wall of Sound was assembled at A&M. We were in the big studio, and the lot was buzzing with the name John Lennon. We worked there for about a week and then moved to the Record Plant for a few nights. Everyone was totally immersed in the project. This was Phil Spector at his greatest. The material and the band were synched beautifully.

I found John Lennon to be rather shy and unassuming. I would usually get to the studio early to check my drum setup, and each night John would already be there tuning up and going over his material. We had nice long talks about the business and all the records that had helped shape his musical career. He thanked me for working with him and said that he had been a fan, and confessed that most of his favorites were "your" West Coast records that he had grown up with.

John was going through a rough period at the time. He was estranged from Yoko, unhappy and drinking a lot, and Julian was with him. My son David was with me, and our situations were similar. Julian was only about 12 or 13, as I remember, and he wanted to play drums. The four of us met for lunch one day in Hollywood and had a beautiful time – just fathers and sons.

The last session I did with Phil and John was the last time I saw either of them. John went back to New York, made his great comeback, and the ensuing tragedy is still with all of us. Donna calls from time to time to say hello from Phil, and we've all begged him to come out of retirement to do an all-star Phil Spector Revue. If he ever does pull us all together again, it'll be a show to end all shows. Phil never did do anything small.

8

The Sinatras

Thanks to my touring and recording in the late '50s with Tommy Sands, I had been quickly baptized into rock and roll. I also had received my Screen Actors Guild card and had landed some film parts. With the demos and smaller studio calls, I was logging experience for the more coveted big jobs. After the long crawling period, I was finally entering the walking stage of my career.

I had been alternating between touring with Patti Page and working with The Diamonds, getting more Big Band chops in order to compete on any level as a professional drummer. I figured I had to know as much as possible to be successful in this business.

In the middle of all this activity, I got my first Nancy Sinatra call. By this time I had a couple of gold records under my belt and wasn't a complete unknown. I hadn't seen Nancy since she and Tommy were together, and I was very excited to meet up with her again. I had always enjoyed her company when she was a kid, but now she was grown up and doing her own thing. When we cut *These Boots Are Made for Walkin'*, it really put her on the map as an international star. Now it was Nancy's turn to go out on the road. Little by little, I had begun to accumulate a small fortune working in the studios. I had become first-call for many of the producers and top groups. Consequently, I turned down numerous big acts who asked me to tour. It was impossible to go out on the road when my real gold mine was in the Hollywood studios. In my own mind I was still Harold Belsky, an impoverished kid from the Jewish ghetto, and I wanted the financial security that was coming my way.

I had seen many session musicians take a short tour gig and

return to town with no jobs waiting. Going out on tours would have jeopardized my standing in the studio community.

But Nancy was different. She made me an offer that I just couldn't refuse, plain and simple. She left room for me to commute back to the studios to keep my name in the running for good sessions. She also wanted her "drummer man" in Las Vegas. I melted without resistance and off we went.

Nancy's show at Caesar's Palace was an incredible spectacle. It was the talk of Vegas and I felt great just being a small part of it. Ed Sullivan came to town and decided that Nancy's show would be a good Sunday night Ed Sullivan Show special. The entire hour was dedicated to Nancy, something previously unheard of. It was a great thrill for all of us who were involved. At the time, Nancy was going with Hugh Lambert, a top show producer, and this was his baby.

We also did shows at the Sahara and the Hilton International, and each one was more spectacular than the last. Then, out of the blue, Nancy decided it was time to retire and raise her family. I was sad to see the run with Nancy end, but I had a feeling I would be seeing more of the family.

Sure enough, I received a call to go to Western Studios in Hollywood on July 17, 1964. This was the big one I had been waiting for – a date with the Chairman of the Board.

Ernie Freeman was conducting, and Sid Sharp and his string section were there in all their glory. It was a Who's Who of the top studio players: Glen Campbell, Tommy Tedesco and Al Casey on guitars, Lincoln Mayorga on piano and Gary Coleman, Emil Richards and Julius Wechter on percussion. Donny Lanier (known as "Dirt" to all his friends) was the favorite rhythm guitarist. Joe Mondragon was on upright bass and Chuck Berghoffer played the Fender. Gene Cipriano and Plas Johnson blew sax. There was lots of brass, and with the French horn players and harpist it looked like a symphony orchestra waiting in the big Studio One.

Producer Jimmy Bowen had been working with "The Rat Pack" one by one. He was turning out hit after hit for Warner Brothers/Reprise with the likes of Sammy Davis, Jr., Dean Martin and Joey Bishop.

Jimmy was the golden goose of the day, and I was fortunate to be his steady drummer.

We all arrived about 6 p.m. and, as was the custom with Mr. Sinatra, we rehearsed the material for about three hours before his arrival. There was a solid wave of energy; electricity buzzed in that studio. This date brought together the absolute creme de la creme of studio players, and everyone was fired up. Frank was a man who did very few takes and the band had to be ready to do it right when the red light went on. Newcomers like myself, who had never recorded with Frank, were in a state of euphoria. Even the old-timers felt the buzz.

The first number we rehearsed was *Softly As I Leave You*, a gorgeous song and a beautiful arrangement. The singers knew instinctively what Ernie wanted and how to phrase his choral accompaniments perfectly. Barney Kessel's wife BJ. (who I always called "Diamond Lil") was there with Jackie Ward, Sally Stevens, Johnny Manne, Ron Hicklin, Alan Capps – all top studio singers.

The rehearsals went well and everyone was ready to go. There was no screwing around this night. No jokes, peanut throwing or beer drinking. The guys in our Wrecking Crew of young session players even dressed up for the occasion – no Levi's and tom T-shirts. The studio engineering crew, with Eddie Brackett at the controls, had everything ready. Every mic had been tested and tested again. Each line to the booth had been double-checked. Every squeaky chair had been replaced. Frank didn't stand for any incompetency or breakdown delays. The security guards, hired for the evening, were strategically stationed around the studio, inside and out. The band was tuned to perfection.

Then the big moment arrived. The back door opened, and Sarge Weiss led the entourage into the studio. Third or fourth in line was Frank, wearing one of his famous hats. In front of Frank walked his latest flame, Mia Farrow. They converged in the booth and all was deathly quiet for a couple of minutes. We sat motionless, waiting for the moment of truth. Frank walked casually into the studio and started greeting the familiar faces, cracking jokes and being as friendly as your best buddy. The place was absolutely lit up with a glow I had never experienced before. Those blue eyes sparkled, and his broad smile warmed the whole place.

It had been five years since I had last seen Frank, and I never expected him to recognize me, but he walked right over to my drum booth and said, "Hi, Blainey." Frank owned Reprise Records, and I had done the dates for Nancy as well as for many of his other artists, so he was aware of my work. Still, I was honored to get a personal greeting from the man of the hour. Then Frank said, "Let's make a record, Ernie." He sang his buns off, of course, and everyone played and sang their best ever. It was a very special night.

Every session with Frank Sinatra seemed to be a milestone in my studio career. He had a commanding presence and a magical energy that put the pressure on, but inspired like nothing else. I was called in for some of his biggest records, including his 1966 Grammy Record of the Year, *Strangers in the Night*. For that date, I simply took the Phil Spector beat that had worked so well before and gave it a new twist for Frank. Bump, bump bump, bang! There were many more – *That's Life, Something Stupid* (with Nancy) – but that first session was the "gasser," as Frank would say. I'll always treasure the Sinatra magic.

9

Making Waves with the Beach Boys

My first session with the Beach Boys was in early '63. We did a record called *Olly, Olly, Oxen Free*. Brian Wilson was just a skinny young kid who sat at the piano and played chords. He didn't seem to be able to play melodies the way most jazzers were playing piano, comping with the left hand and playing melodies and ad lib lines with the right. Brian was comping with both hands and singing the melody, humming as he played, because the words weren't written yet. I didn't realize that his twohanded camping with all ten fingers was fanning the chord structure for his vocals that would follow with the group.

This was the beginning of Brian's rise to success, and since most of us were just starting out as regular session musicians, we became his team. We wanted to be the number one musicians in the studios and we didn't question the arranger/composer. We were getting steady work, and when I got a call from a new leader it was another notch on my drumsticks.

Surfing was the rage, and the whole world was looking to California for the music of summer. What better name for a group than the Beach Boys? They symbolized every teenage dream of freedom, fun, romance, and sunshine.

The sessions were a lot of fun. We worked at Gold Star first, where I had done all the Spector dates. Later we moved to United/ Western, then to Brian's house and even later to their Brothers Studio in Santa Monica. Glen Campbell, as well as Jan and Dean sang on the records (the Beach Boys used to sing on Jan and Dean's records, too). There was a great feeling of camaraderie in the early days of rock and roll. It was common for various acts to join in on other artists' records.

When we did the first Beach Boys dates at Gold Star, it was no different than working for Phil Spector or Herb Alpert. It was another date at the magical studio that was putting out hit after hit. The Beach Boys were starting to make some noise on the charts, and these sessions were some of the many that included The Wrecking Crew.

Brian was playful and always had a smile on his face, but there was nothing wishy-washy about the way he worked. He was very serious when he sat down at the piano. There was no searching around. He would play exactly what he wanted and there was no experimentation.

Part of The Wrecking Crew was always with Brian in the studio – usually Carol Kaye or Ray Pohlman on bass, Tommy Tedesco on guitar, along with Bill Pittman and Glen Campbell. Oftentimes Billy Strange and Lyle Ritz were there. At Gold Star, Stan Ross handled the knobs in the booth, and at Western it was always Chuck Britz. We had Don Randi on piano and Steve Douglas with his mighty tenor sax sitting next to Jay Migliori. Brian usually had a chord chart and we all made our own parts. When copying machines started coming on the market, Brian brought in his chart and sent it to the office for more copies. They were simple chord charts, and we all filled in what Brian wanted. We'd run it down a few times, make a few minor adjustments and the old 2-track would be punched up. In a couple of takes we'd have it.

Brian didn't believe in a lot of takes, but he did believe in a lot of sessions. We often did small segments of a song and that was it after just a few takes. But other times we'd rehearse for hours while Brian got the sound he wanted in the booth. *Good Vibrations* took many, many sessions with many segments recorded and rerecorded. He was a fanatic about having everything perfect. He wanted spontaneity but he wanted a perfect take. That's one of the big things you learn in the studios. It's the sign of a great actor or artist of any kind – making it sound like it just came off the top of your head after you've been rehearsing it for hours, days or even months.

In the early sessions, we had no idea what the finished product would sound like. We recorded basic tracks, bits and pieces, and that was that. Sometimes we heard rough vocals in the studio, but the Beach Boys didn't really want anybody around when they did the finished vocals. Then we started hearing the records on the radio and realized what was going on. The combination of Brian's vision and the painstaking work on the songs created something that took pop music to a new level.

My particular sound for Brian was basically the Phil Spector sound with a few minor changes. For Spector the snare sound had to be very high and tight to cut through the "Wall" and do all of the craziness that happened on the fades. The toms were left midrange, and I always played the snare and the floor tom in unison to strengthen the back beat sound. I rarely used cymbals or played hi hat eighths. For Brian I modified the snare to a lower sound combined with the floor tom and he loved it.

Afterwards, I would overdub percussion effects. I was invited to experiment, and I don't ever remember Brian telling me not to play anything I thought might work. He wanted a good back beat, and beyond that whatever I wanted to do was okay. Percussionists have had little toys around for years, but you never used claves or shakers unless it was a Latin tune, for example. I started using effects on the sessions and they usually ended up on the records.

Brian's father, Murray Wilson, was often at the dates and his presence caused a few clashes. Brian knew exactly what he was going for, but Murray was usually thinking in opposite terms. After a while Brian barred his dad from the sessions, and then everything was smooth sailing. But Murray came on the scene again, this time with his own group, The Sunrays. He was determined to show Brian he could do it. Murray was quite a colorful character. Before each session with The Rays, he said a prayer and then passed out $2 bills to all of us for good luck. But The Sunrays never really happened.

I am often asked what Dennis Wilson's feelings were about me playing the drums. After all, he was the group's drummer. Dennis and I were good friends. He admired and respected my technique, and Dennis was no fool. The popularity of the Beach Boys was paying for all of his whims – motorcycles, boats, women and fast cars. He was living the good life and I don't think that he really wanted to be in the studios as much as in the early days. But in later years, Dennis became very involved in the Brothers Studio complex. He even hired me to play on his solo album for Warner Brothers. Dennis also played great piano, maybe better than drums. Don't get me wrong; he could never really be replaced by anyone else. He was the consummate Beach Boy. He was the only real surfer of the group, and it showed. He had all of the women going crazy while he pounded the drums on stage. (I was part of one of their Hawaiian shows and saw how the audience reacted to Dennis. The Hawaiians obviously loved all the Beach Boys, but

Dennis in particular.) I think the least known Beach Boy, Bruce Johnston, was probably the most talented of the gang, along with Brian, of course. Bruce (who came along later and isn't related to the others) and I first met when he was playing the organ on a session. I couldn't get over his incredible touch. He was a real unknown to The Wrecking Crew, but you could hear this mountain of talent pouring out of the Hammond B-3. I knew it wouldn't be long before he would be a star in his own right. I always thought that if Bruce had gone out on his own instead of joining the Beach Boys, he would have hit solo stardom.

Mike Love and Al Jardine were Beach Boys from the start. They had their squabbles like every other family, but they were always respectful of the musicians making their records. They weren't around as much as Brian, but their distinctive voices were an irreplaceable part of that Beach Boys sound.

Mike Love was the onstage comedian of the group, and the kids loved him. Brother Carl Wilson was usually at all of the sessions playing bass or guitar, and helping arrange and compose. Carl was a very quiet and determined youngster. Everything he did was well thought out, and when he made a suggestion it usually worked perfectly. Carl also had some good musical training, and it showed.

The Beach Boys didn't really impress me at first. I had done sessions with the Hi-Los, the Four Freshmen and the Four Preps, among others, and I thought Brian was copying these other singers. Boy, was I wrong! Brian's roots were the Hi-Los and the Freshmen, but the Beach Boys were so intense in their vocal structures that within weeks I realized their sound was something very different. The Beach Boys were taking what were then simple rock and roll chords and making them much more sophisticated. And who could have imagined there would be hit songs about surfing and hot rods? No one had done what the Beach Boys were doing, and the fans loved it. So did The Wrecking Crew. We knew we were making some history.

I felt good about being part of their music. It's what I had been working for all my life. A lot of the older Hollywood studio musicians said they wouldn't play that stuff. They packed their bags, and a lot of guys left the business forever. But some of them got smart. Players who had been badmouthing The Wrecking Crew started hanging around to find out what was going on. I'd hear things like, "Hey, I thought it was just a stupid rock and roll thing, a fad. I had no idea." Brian was a thinker, a creator, and with the bucks the Beach Boys were making, the sky was the limit. One time we were in the middle of a session and Brian called me in to listen to a playback.

A business manager was also in the booth trying to talk to him about the excess money that was sitting in Brian's Sea of Tunes publishing company and how something had to be done with it. Brian kept telling this guy to shut up and finally yelled, "Just do whatever you have to do and leave us alone!" This man wrote out a check for a half-million bucks and Brian signed it. He was glued to the playback. His eyes and ears were on the studio speakers and he just signed the check like he was off on another planet.

Brian liked to call me into the booth to listen to playbacks. He wanted to know if the track was in perfect tempo and steady. Phil Spector used to call me in all the time as well – it became a regular request with producers, because the basic tracks were the foundation on which the rest of the material was built. Every hit record was an investment in my career, and if I had missed a beat it would be hard to live down.

The sessions for *Pet Sounds* were especially entertaining. It was really a big, long party recorded in the larger Studio Two at Western, so there was enough room for all the friends and relatives. People were singing along and clapping, and I think the tape machine was left on most of the time to catch the spontaneity. The sessions weren't exactly free-form, because there was an organizational concept, but there was a lot of room for surprises.

After Brian married Marilyn they moved into the Bellagio house in Bel-Air. Everything seemed great. Brian immediately had the house painted purple and the wrath of the community came down on him. There was an ordinance that houses could not be changed from their original color. Brian had to have the entire house repainted. That was two paint jobs in a matter of days. And we're not talking about a small A-frame house down the block. This was an estate in Bel-Air. The next move seemed to be logical. Brian had a magnificent den with a beautiful rock fireplace. It soon became the new Beach Boys studio. He spent a fonune having a booth put in upstairs overlooking the den. I think it was 1967. From then on it seemed like everything started going downhill for the Beach Boys. As with most record acts, the fans were on to the next craze. The record buyers were growing up and going off in other directions to new groups and new sounds.

When we'd record at the house in Bel-Air, we'd go through the big iron gates and set up in the converted den that had become the new studio. A big piece of board covered up the fireplace so the sound wouldn't go up the chimney. The control room was above us, with small slits for the engineer to look through. It was an alienating environment, and stranger still when Brian disappeared from the scene. If we asked what was going on, we were told that Brian was elsewhere. It was all hush-hush and mysterious, but we continued recording. I don't think anything major came out of the sessions.

With every passing day Brian was having more mental problems, problems we knew nothing about. He got into meditation and I don't know what all. We'd catch a glimpse of him in pajamas and he didn't recognize anyone. He gained about 100 pounds and was almost unrecognizable. His hair was shoulder-length and his whiskers made him look like an old man, unkempt and in a general state of dishevelment. He reminded me of the old wrestler, "Man Mountain Dean." It was sad for all of us to watch.

Several years later I got a call from Terry Melcher. He was going to do a date at RCA with Brian and wanted the old gang there. It was more therapeutic than creative, just to see how Brian would react. When Brian arrived he was even heavier and his hair was longer. He acted strange and kept shaking his head, as if a nervous tick had overtaken him. He entered this massive studio and walked to the piano and started comping the intro to *Good Vibrations*. He kept looking over at me as if I were a stranger, muttering, "Do you know this song?" I almost cried, but I managed to keep my composure and said, "Sure, Brian. One of my favorites." He kept looking around the room at other people. They were all old friends, but he was squinting at them as if they were strangers. He got up after a few minutes and walked out. We were all speechless. Brian had really hit bottom.

In 1982, I got a call from Chuck Britz: "Brian wants to record!" I entered Western Studio One expecting the worst. Brian walked in, shook hands with the old Wrecking Crew and we realized we were witnessing a miracle. He had lost what seemed like a couple of hundred pounds and was his old self. He gave everybody the chord charts and we started working. He stopped once in a while and gave note changes to the horns. We practically had tears in our eyes, we were so happy. He was the old Brian Wilson. We did three sessions and it was like old times.

10

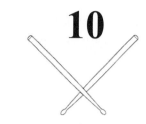

Up And Down with Jan and Dean

I had spent most of my life in ghettos and tenements, but now I could afford a full-blown 25-room house in the Hollywood Hills – a mansion with nearly an acre of land. I was five minutes from every studio in Hollywood and not more than 20 minutes from any of the movie studios.

Living close to Hollywood was a great plus for me. I soon learned that when a 20 or 30-piece orchestra was sitting in a studio and the drummer hadn't shown up ten or 15 minutes into a session, it was time to call a replacement in a hurry. Because I was the closest and was getting a name for myself, I was always the first one called. If I was at home, I could be at the studio in five minutes, sitting at the other drummer's kit, ready to do the date or at least sit in until he showed up. Each time it happened to me I did, in fact, get to finish the date, and was paid premium for doing it.

When I got a personal call from Jan Berry of Jan and Dean, I had very little knowledge of the duo. Jan was a promising composer/ arranger/singer. He was young and handsome and studying medicine. Dean Torrence, who was even more striking, if that was possible, was studying architecture. They were just a couple of college kids from decent middle-class homes. Jan and Dean personified the California Dream: sports cars, blond hair, tall and muscular builds; the epitome of the young surfer image. Although they hadn't yet become major stars, it was written all over them. When we walked through the parking lot at United/ Western Studios, we would pass school girls coming home, and these young kids would swoon shamelessly, do double takes and often follow them to their cars. It was amazing. I had experienced this phenomenon working with Tommy Sands, but he was already an established teen idol. Jan and Dean were just starting out.

Well, within a couple of years they had become stars, just as many of us predicted, thanks to the success of *Surf City, Little Old Lady From Pasadena*, and some other million-sellers. By then they had beautiful Bel-Air homes and everything that comes with wealth and stardom. After playing on their records, I was asked to do a couple of road trips with them, and I never saw such a crowd scene in my life. Everyone stood for the entire show, screaming with delight and crying with anxiety. Many of the girls would collapse from the hysteria and be sent to hospitals in ambulances.

Jan was a hard-head, Dean was a softy. Where Jan was often belligerent, Dean was always soft-spoken. You could almost see a halo floating over Dean's long, blond hair. With Jan, you could imagine the horns that went along with his sometimes devilish manner. But we all got along great, and fun was the bottom line. I couldn't wait to get out on the road and do concerts with them.

I remember once we were working in Seattle for Pat O'Day and Tom Hulett, two very prominent promoters of the day. When we arrived at the auditorium, the crowds were massive. It took an entire team of cops to get us through the mob and up to the backstage area where kids were standing 50 deep. The cops left us there, so we did our best to get through and pushed our way to the private door. We started pounding to get in, but these backstage cops were used to hearing pounding and nobody answered the door.

Jan and Dean were both wearing their stage costumes: surfer T-shirts that made them look just like the kids who were trying to get in. After pounding and screaming at the top of my lungs, a cop finally opened the door to peek out. I told him that these were the stars of the show and that we had to get in. But the cop didn't believe me.

That's when Jan stepped in and started swearing at this big policeman. The fists started flying, and the cop had Jan on the ground and handcuffed in nothing flat. He called for a black-and-white to take him downtown. "You're under arrest, punk, and that's that!" And through it all, Jan was calling this big ox every name in the book. I did my best to convince this officer that if Jan was arrested there would be a riot the likes of which Seattle had never seen, but I was talking to deaf ears.

I somehow managed to get Dean and me through the door and went looking for Pat O'Day. I found him in the production office, and he came out and finally convinced the sergeant that there would be a major riot if the show was canceled. The show went on as scheduled, and it turned out to be an incredible performance.

After the concert we all gathered at a dinner house where the sergeant and his men were the guests of Pat O'Day, Tom Hulett, and Jan and Dean. The good policeman couldn't wait to get autographed pictures and albums for his kids, plus a few photos taken with Jan and Dean for his den.

It wasn't too long after that explosive evening that Paramount Pictures signed the duo to a film contract. They were going to be the new Laurel and Hardy. Jan and Dean had both spent time in Santa Monica with Stan Laurel shortly before his death. They were Laurel and Hardy freaks and fashioned a lot of their comedy antics on classic routines.

On the first day of shooting, they were on location in the San Fernando Valley rehearsing a train sequence. Two trains were to come together while Jan and Dean were walking on the railroad tracks. This was actually to be the last scene of the film, the closing shot. There would be a narrow escape for the kids as the two trains slammed on their brakes and stopped within inches of each other. The rehearsals went off without a hitch, and then the director called for action.

The cameras started rolling and the trains approached. Some-how, the brakes went out on one of these monstrous locomotives, and the trains smashed together. It was like an atomic blast as thousands of tons of steel collided. People went flying into the air and landed like rag dolls, many of them unconscious. Dean had managed to get off the tracks before the crash, but Jan wasn't so lucky. He looked at his leg and saw that it had been nearly severed by a wheel. With blood gush-ing from veins and arteries just below the knee, Jan put his medical school training to work. He fashioned a tourniquet from his belt and, in the midst of all the confusion, dragged himself almost a quarter-mile across a desert area to the highway and flagged down a passing motorist.

The driver rushed Jan to the Northridge Hospital, and the first thing he heard was the doctor mumbling something about amputation. Jan gave strict orders that he would not allow an amputation until his doctor could be called in for a consultation. Jan's orthopedic doctor, Dr. Robert Grant, was also his professor at UClA. When Grant arrived from the West Hills hospital, he told Jan that no one would amputate. And with that, Jan collapsed. With his leg in a cast, he went back to college, but it was still onward and upward for Jan and Dean. Through all the time we spent recording, overdubbing, mixing and the like, the two were still students doing their school thing by day and recording by night. The Paramount movie deal was scrapped, but 20th Century Fox began talking to them about some other film possibilities. After all, these kids were hot on the music scene and seemed destined for movies.

Jan called me one day and said, "Hal, how'd you like to be a movie star with us?" In a couple of days I received a script titled "Jan and Dean on the Road." It was a clever pilot to be directed by William Asher (of the Lucy shows and Bewitched). My role was "Clobber," the drummer (talk about typecasting). I had worked for some years before at Paramount as an extra and a bit player. I was familiar with the film business and had done photo doubling for Sal Mineo and some stunts for Yul Brynner. I really enjoyed working in films, and the salaries were great.

After a few meetings with Asher at Fox, everything was set. The Jan and Dean show was to be a weekly series about their life on the road and all the trials and tribulations of a rock act. There would be a lot of comedy and pathos, and, of course, plenty of rock and roll. We would also be recording the music for the show. The pilot called for a number of locations all over the country, with a huge concert in San Diego to wind it up. It was a couple of months' work, and we were being treated like royalty by one of the biggest studios in the world. Even my wife was along to enjoy the ride. This, was really the big time – limos, make-up men, publicity shots – the works.

Our first day of shooting was at a special section of TWA's terminal at LA. airport, where they had mock-ups of their planes. As my limo approached the area I saw a lot of police cars with their red lights flashing. I thought maybe there had been a plane crash, but no, Jan and Dean had decided to come out early that morning and race their cars all over the runways before anyone else arrived. These dummies almost shut down the picture before it began. They were told they were going to jail, and it took a lot of convincing by Bill Asher and the powers at Fox to cool out the police. Jan and Dean had a knack for effortlessly getting into trouble.

Well, we finally got things straightened out and began working. It was a ball and went well from that point forward. My big part usually consisted of their "manager" asking, "Clobb, have you got the music?" to which I replied, "Have I got the music?!" We shot at airports all over the country and the "manager" would keep asking me if I had the music. I would always answer, "Have I got the music?!" After a few more exchanges I would be running off the plane and Jan and Dean would ask, "Where ya going, Clobb?" I would deadpan to the camera and say, "I forgot the music." This was my big gag.

Each night after our shooting was done I sat up half the night with Jan and helped him cram for his medical finals that were coming up as soon as we got back to LA. I coached him on pharmaceutical formulas, the names of the bones in the body, etc. I was fascinated by this side of Jan's life and it amazed me how well he could study both medicine and his script. He seemed to have a photographic memory.

We wound up in San Diego for the final concert sequence and did an unbelievable live show. I got most of the session players from The Wrecking Crew flown down from L.A. and acted as bandleader. It was a wild time. There were thousands of screaming kids and it was good money for everyone.

We went to a couple of screenings and everyone agreed that the show would be a hit and we would all be gainfully employed at 20th Century-Fox for some years. As soon as the pilot was in the can we started to record again.

A typical session with Jan and Dean began with a call from Jan asking me to get the Crew together. I would then get Arlyn Henry, the owner of Arlyn's Answering Service, to call the gang. Arlyn and her girls used to put out the contractor's calls because we contractors, being a busy bunch of people, could not sit for a day or two by the phone waiting for everyone to get their messages and call back, accepting or rejecting the session. With Jan it was usually, "I want to record tomorrow – any problem?"

Plenty of problems! Getting seven or eight busy guys together for a session was almost impossible, especially getting Earl Palmer and me scheduled to do double drums. We were the busiest drummers in town, each of us working four or five dates a day, so we usually had to make it a late session – very late. I usually tried to get Earl on the phone personally to coordinate our schedules before having Arlyn contact the rest of the band.

The double drums was an idea that Jan had because he used to like to overdub a second track of drums exactly like the first. This presented a lot of problems, so he finally settled for the obvious: two drummers. Earl and I played everything in unison – every fill, every backbeat. We rehearsed our parts as one, and talked about what we'd play on each drum: the toms here, the snare here, etc. I don't think anyone used dual drummers on tracks before that, and it really started something.

The rest of the session players on those dates usually consisted of Glen Campbell, Billy Strange and Tommy Tedesco on guitars; Bill Pittman on Danelectro bass; Carol Kaye or Ray Pohlman on Fender bass; and Larry Knechtel, Glen D. Hardin or Don Randi on piano. Other players we used frequently included Jimmy Bond, Red Callender and Lyle Ritz on upright bass; Joe Osborne on electric bass; Al Casey, David Cohen, Michael Deasy and Don Peake on guitars; and Julius Wechter on percussion. Liberty Records spent a fortune on these two hitmakers and was surrounding them with the best musicians in Hollywood.

The sessions were always fun, with many ending in the early morning hours and finding us in various states of giddiness and exhaustion. I remember one night in particular when someone had brought in a couple cases of beer and five pounds of shelled peanuts. By about two in the morning everyone was feeling pretty good. Then Glen Campbell started throwing peanut shells at Billy Strange, who in turn started throwing beer cans at Tedesco. Before you knew it, the mini-war was on and everyone joined in with beer cans and peanut shells flying all over the place. Between the flying debris and the passing of gas in that tiny Studio Three at Western, it smelled like the gas company had broken a main and it looked like the circus had left town without cleaning up. What a mess. That night, The Wrecking Crew really lived up to its name.

During this time, Jan was in finals and about to start interning. After being in school all day, he'd record half the night and study the other half. I knew that it was taking its toll, but I never knew how much. Jan called one morning and said that he'd see me that night after school. I was just leaving for work, and he was on his way to the draft board and then classes. He was getting a medical student draft deferment from Uncle Sam. It was the last time we would speak for months to come.

About ten in the morning one of the engineers came into the studio and told us that he had just heard the news that Jan had been killed. Jesus. We were all in a state of shock. I made a few calls and finally got Lou Adler, who said that he had heard about the accident but that Jan was alive – barely – at the UCLA Medical Center. They couldn't tell us anything except that he was undergoing brain surgery.

There were many accounts of the accident, but the official story seems to be that Jan made a turn from a stop sign in Beverly Hills, and somehow his Corvette Stingray slid under the back of a parked truck. This was "Dead Man's Curve" for real. His skull was cracked open, and the police pronounced him dead at the scene. After the paramedics arrived, they found weak signs of life and rushed him to the UCLA Med Center, where the neurosurgeons took over. The doctors didn't give Jan much hope; they doubted he would ever come out of his deep coma. He was in intensive care for a long, long time and then finally put into a private room, where he remained comatose, kept alive by IVs in both arms, oxygen tubes in the nose and a 24-hour nurse sitting with him. His folks had already been through unimaginable hard times – they had lost a daughter in a swimming pool accident and another son in a mountain climbing accident. Faced with this disaster – just a few months after Jan had gotten out of his leg cast – they selflessly spent most of their time by his side.

None of us expected Jan to live. Every conversation in the studios turned to Jan Berry. Each day seemed bleaker, but then one day word came that he had opened his eyes for the first time. He had come out of his coma!

I started visiting the hospital as much as possible. I'd just sit there next to the bed, talk to Jan as if he were completely coherent, and he'd look at me with a blank stare. One Sunday afternoon I was sitting there talking about records and what I had done during the week. It was my usual conversation with him and, of course, I wasn't getting any response. I bent over to say "See you next time," when his arm came up and hugged my neck and pulled me down against his face. This was his first movement since the accident. I called everyone waiting outside in the hallway, and they all came running. It was quite a day. I cried like a baby, and so did everyone else.

Little by little, Jan began to recover mentally and physically. His entire right side was paralyzed – right arm, right leg, even his right eye. Sandy Melvoin, his nurse, moved into the Bel-Air home and worked full time. The best specialists in the world were consulted, but still he was given no real hope for a full recovery because he had sustained so much brain damage. He could speak only very slowly, almost like a 3-year-old. He remembered nothing. His music was gone. His medical knowledge was gone. He was unfamiliar with his surroundings. He didn't comprehend any of the records we played for him. It was total amnesia, which was a very sad thing to see. He had grown very thin and didn't look anything like the young, handsome man we had known.

Eventually, Jan was sent to Rancho Los Amigos, a special hospital for therapy. After months as a regular patient, and then an outpatient, he began to walk – a sad, sick person's walk, but at least a walk. He got around with a crutch and dragged his right foot behind him, while his right arm just hung from the shoulder socket.

Then he started remembering things. It was only little things at first, but soon his memory started coming back in big chunks. We started talking music again, and the day came when he wanted to start recording.

Jan was feeling pretty good now. He was sometimes childlike, but he remembered more and more, and finally started to laugh again. The doctors at Rancho Los Amigos embedded an electrical impulse device in his right leg to help stimulate movement, and he wore a small control box on his belt. He was so proud of that. He'd demonstrate the magic box by showing us his dragging leg and then, after switching on the box, his leg would straighten and he could walk by himself. Before long he was driving a car again.

Dean, in the meantime, had developed a successful graphics company and had set his sights on a new career. Jan continued to improve and eventually he and Dean were even able to perform again, though the days of superstardom were gone.

11

Monkee Business!

The date was June 10, 1966. The place was RCA Studios in Hollywood. Leon Russell was on piano, and I remember him smiling quietly to himself, wondering how they could have used a name like "The Monkees." It sounded like a show biz hoax. The Monkees?

Jeff Barry produced the sessions for Don Kirshner Productions. Jeff had been contracted to produce this "band" of four youngsters who would be America's wacky television answer to The Beatles. Screen Gems and Columbia Pictures were setting up the biggest promotional push in the history of the studio, and they kept these kids running from wardrobe sessions to TV interviews to screen tests to the rehearsals for the TV series.

At the time, we had no idea of the impact these four kids would have on the world of entertainment. I guess we should have suspected something, though, since everything The Wrecking Crew recorded had been turning to gold. That's why we were here.

When we did meet the group, we were surprised. They were highly intelligent and well-manicured. They were typical products of the times: young, vibrant, long-haired, cute and funny as hell. It was joke after joke, and these kids could handle themselves like the top comedians of the day.

I've often been asked how some of the different groups we worked with felt about a team of pros making their records. I don't think they minded at all. After all, while we were making 35 bucks for making their records, they were making $35,000 for performing them onstage. It was just the nature of the business and we figured that most people understood, although for obvious reasons, our behind-the-scenes role was not publicized. In many cases, the stars were too busy touring to spend the weeks and weeks in the studio it usually takes to make a great record. They were on the road or making films and couldn't stop to make all the records that had to be released on schedule. The Wrecking Crew was called in to make those records.

Toward the middle of 1967, our idyllic studio relationship was briefly jeopardized by what became known to some as "The Monkee Scandal.' A fan magazine, obviously out for blood, did a slashing article on the group and "exposed" how The Monkees didn't make their own records. This revelation shook the foundations of The Monkees' media machine just when the band's weekly TV show was hot, their records were consistently at the top of the charts and their concert appearances were always sold out. They had achieved genuine superstardom, and now a magazine was trying to destroy it all. No question about it, there was trouble in paradise.

I remember one day in Studio A at RCA we were making Monkees records in a studio the size of an aircraft hangar, with all the doors locked and "closed session" signs all over. Next door, in Studio C, The Monkees sat at their instruments making music for the press. The studio bosses had set up the session to squelch the ugly rumors, and the boys gave a convincing performance. Eventually, things cooled down, and later that year I got a call from band member Michael Nesmith (he of the drawl and knit cap) asking me to contract some musicians for a few dates. This was a common request. I had been contracting for all the guys in the group as they developed their solo careers and did the same for many musicians in Hollywood. Not only had I established myself as a session drummer, but also as a contractor whose deals were honest. I made sure no one got cheated when they worked for me – this in a business well known for cheats. There were unreported dates, unpaid dates, forgotten overtime, and doubling and overdubbing that were mysteriously forgotten. Fortunately, The Wrecking Crew was on top and could weed out the grafters. Our answer to the sleazy ones was: "Sorry, we're booked this month." We even gave a list of cheaters to our answering service, and when someone on the list called, the answer was: "Sorry, they're out of town."

Anyway, Michael called me and laid out the plans for a super session, the likes of which had never been seen in Hollywood – a session that would be done on Saturday and Sunday, known as "golden time" for union members. It was a date that we'd never forget – catered with Chasen's silver service and a gathering of musicians that was unbelievable. Shorty Rogers was doing the arrangements, and what a call it was: ten trumpets, ten trombones, ten saxophones, five percussionists, two drummers, four piano players, seven guitars, four Fender bass players, four upright basses, and on and on. It sounded like World

War III. In fact, Nesmith was going to call it that, but changed it to *The Pacific Ocean* and ultimately called it *The Wichita Train Whistle.*

The town was buzzing with excitement about the session; no one could believe that it could get on tape. I was the envy of all the major contractors in town; many of them called and made nice offers to take over the job. Everyone wanted to be on the session.

The dates arrived: November 18 and 19, 1967. Shorty had worked his ass off and came up with brilliant arrangements. Earl Palmer and I were on cloud nine, because it was a drummer's dream to be able to kick this gigantic band in the butt. We all took a lot of breaks during the recording to stuff our faces with gourmet chow. Gene Cipriano, the saxophone/oboist, got his reeds jammed with caviar. We were all like kids in a candy store. Two of The Wrecking Crew trumpet players came close to exploding. Finally, I asked Michael why he had called for such a costly session. He explained that Uncle Sam was about to remove 50 grand from his pocket and, instead of paying the taxes, he decided to spend it on a raucous write-off. So Nesmith made his peace with the IRS, our union pension plans got a healthy shot in the arm, and everyone was happy.

(The Musician's Union pension plan calls for members to get an extra 10 percent above their gross salary for a job. The pension money is paid by the employer to the union fund and goes directly into an account with the musician's name on it. After 30 years or so, it can really add up and help out in your old age. That's why it's so imponant for union members to be sure there is a contract on every job and that the pension gets paid. Whether it's records, TV, movies, commercials, or even nightclubs and casuals, there must be pension requirements, but it's important to check it out. We're all terminal in this business. When it's over, it's over. Unless you want to spend the rest of your life working honky-tonks for low pay, see that your pension is taken care of.)

The Nesmith dates came off without a hitch. It was the greatest party I had ever been invited to. Two days of Chasen's food, and more music than you could expect to play in a lifetime. It was fun and games all the way through, and when the last note was played, Tommy Tedesco threw his guitar up in the air (about 40 feet), and we all stood there frozen as it crashed down on the floor of the studio and splintered to bits. He had the pieces mounted and framed, and it hangs over his favorite poker chair to this day, bringing back all the wild memories of our times with The Monkees.

12

Jimmy Webb and
The Fifth Dimension

The first time I saw this tall, skinny Oklahoma kid who had just arrived in Hollywood, I had no idea he would become such a major force in modem music. The teenage Jimmy Webb was in town to record a young singing trio from San Bernardino, where he was living at the time. From the start I knew he had talent, a gift for songwriting I hadn't heard since the days of Cole Porter and the Gershwins.

I first worked with Jimmy at copyist Bob Ross' small home studio near Hollywood and Vine. Bob copied music for all the top arrangers in town and provided the sheet music for many of the major recording sessions.

His studio was actually a converted living room. While we were busy recording, Bob's staff of copyists was working in various rooms throughout the house. It was like a small newspaper office, with people running presses and copying machines all over the place. Some were scribbling away with pens in hand, others were preparing onion skins and pasting up the charts.

Just off the front room, which operated as the reception area, there was an alcove where Lou Halmy sat at a tiny upright piano and copied down songs for people who couldn't read music or didn't have the time to write it down. You sang your songs to Lou and as he whistled each phrase he committed it to paper, adding the chords and the lyrics to fit the melody line. One of Bob's copyists would then put it on onion skin and file it away. Anytime you needed a dozen copies of your song, you called Bob Ross Music Company and the onion skin went into the duplicating machine. An unsung hero, Bob played a part in thousands of hit songs.

After Jimmy introduced his trio of lady singers to me, he explained that it was his first real recording session. He sat at the piano, and as he sang his songs he frequently glanced over to one of the singers. He was obviously in love with this girl, Susie, and had written the songs for her. In fact, just about every major hit he wrote over the next few years was in some way connected with Susie.

Jimmy started commuting to Hollywood every chance he had and made a deal with some people who let him use their studio on a barter basis. He could record as much as he wanted in return for the publishing rights to his songs. It sounded fine to a kid who needed to record and didn't have any money. What he didn't know was that he was giving away a fortune. Most of his early hits are still owned today by those same people. Fortunately, he wrote many more hits and formed his own publishing company, Canopy Productions (named for his *Up, Up, and Away*.)

After Jimmy got free of his initial contracts, he signed a solid deal with Johnny Rivers. Rivers was the owner of Soul City Records. and was an established star in his own right. The Wrecking Crew had been doing his records, and one day he told us he wanted to record one of Jimmy's songs. We were skeptical, because it didn't sound like a rock date and Johnny had been producing rock artists. The singer was Tony Manin, the film and nightclub star. We assembled at Studio Three over at United/Western, Johnny's favorite studio, and recorded *By the Time I Get to Phoenix* in Tony's pop style. Nothing at all happened with the record.

Shortly after that date, Johnny signed up a new group called The Fifth Dimension, a fresh and lively black group that sang in a very pop style, at least to my ears. They were good-looking, had a great sound, and each member had a very distinct personality. When engineer Bones Howe got together with Jimmy and we cut *Up, Up, and Away*; we all knew we had a hit on our hands but we had no idea it would cop the Grammy for Record of the Year (1967). I was especially honored when Jimmy and the group had me take a bow at the awards ceremony.

During that time I was working nonstop in the studios all week and also playing for The Steve Allen Show over at CBS on the weekends. Jazz vibraphonist Terry Gibbs was the bandleader for the show and got me the gig. It was a super band with a great sense of humor, and I was having a ball.

When *Up, Up, and Away* first started making some noise nationally, Steve booked The Fifth Dimension for his show. The group was in heaven when they walked into CBS Television City and stepped onto the Steve Allen stage. Although they weren't yet a household name, they were given the total star treatment, complete with dressing rooms filled with flowers.

My stage position with the TV show's band was in the front, close to Terry (who always had his electric metronome going for each upcoming music cue). The band was isolated for sound just off the seating area, so we were quite a distance from the actual stage action. I had a small monitor in front of me so I could follow the action of the show and do a "ba-dum-dum" on the drums whenever I felt like it. With my monitor and headphones I could see every shot and hear all of the dialog.

I carefully watched the kids as they rehearsed a number a few times. From the look on Steve's face and the reactions of the production people, it was obvious that the Fifth was bombing. They appeared stiff and cold, mostly just scared, but it really looked bad. The talk around the stage was, "What the hell have we booked here?" During a break, I headed for their dressing room, feeling a little like Knute Rockne. "Listen, you guys, what's wrong? You're not movin' and groovin' like you do in the studio. I always see you with your arms around each other, looking at one another and loving each other while you're singing. That's what's missing here today. I'm no director, but I've been watching you all day and you're colder than ice."

I think I shook them up a little. They thanked me and told me how much they appreciated the pep talk. They agreed to give it their best shot and went back onstage. The next runthrough just murdered everyone. Steve couldn't believe it was the same group. The show went ahead as planned, and they were a smash.

Johnny Rivers had Bones Howe engineering all his hits of the day. Bones had a master's degree in electrical engineering and was also a drummer. He not only had the ears of a great engineer, he had incredible coordination. He could mix an entire track as it was being cut live, adding all the studio tricks that would give it a unique sound. Bones was a quiet genius who worked behind the scenes, making major contributions to every project he touched. He rapidly advanced to full-fledged producer/engineer. He did everything himself, eliminating a lot of precious time trying to get an engineer to do it his way. Bones was, and is, a perfectionist.

"Here we go, Belsk – a dozen and four." he'd say to me, meaning that we were about to do take 16. Cry as we might, we gave it our best and always felt better for having done it. Sometimes it was two dozen and four, but still we would do it like it was take one. You can never tell, and things sometimes happen – magical things – when you're caught up in doing a perfect job.

Bones was also a genius with the razor blade and would often take pieces of a song, adding and deleting, and come up with stunning arrangements that weren't there in the beginning. More than once he took my drum licks and made some new piece of music.

Jimmy Webb soon became the goose that laid golden eggs for many artists. With so much new success and wealth, he rented the former Philippine consulate's residence not far from my home in the Hollywood Hills. I used to drop by often, and I couldn't believe what was happening for this 17-year-old kid. Universal Pictures gave him a bungalow on the movie lot for his Canopy offices. He had carte blanche at the studios for recording whatever and whenever he wanted. They even presented him with five gold Cadillacs as an incentive to do his life story – at that tender age! We used to sit around his house building model planes and boats and the phone was constantly ringing. Frank Sinatra calling, Barbra Streisand calling – everybody wanted a piece of Jimmy Webb.

He used to drop in at my house unexpectedly. "You gotta hear this new song," he'd say and sit down at the piano. It was a special privilege to hear his music before anyone else, and I often ended up in tears after hearing his new creations. His talent was simply incredible.

The advertising agency for Chevrolet once asked him to write a commercial. I'll never forget the theme: "Chevy's got the big ones on the way!" Glen Campbell sang it long before he was an established star. During a meeting with the producer up at the house, Jimmy mentioned how much he liked the Corvette and how nice the new station wagon looked, thinking he might refer to them in the commercial. The next morning there was a new Corvette and a new wagon sitting in the driveway, delivered as a gift from Chevrolet. Jimmy was rolling in bucks and the last thing he needed was more cars. He always gave the gift cars away to his friends.

Jimmy played a part in one of the greatest experiences of my life, my first trip to Europe. I received a call from him, now a world traveler, informing me that he had met a film star in London and was writing some special material for him. He asked if I could come to England and help make the record. The star was Richard Harris (affectionately called "the madman" by his friends.) My answer was an emphatic and immediate "yes." Richard had been signed by ABC Dunhill and the project sounded very exciting. But I reminded Jimmy of how busy I was and that I needed a couple of months notice for blocking out the time that he needed. In those days I was usually booked for weeks, if not months, in advance. Jimmy assured me that there would be no problem – he was just starting to write.

A couple of weeks later the phone rang as I was about to leave for the studio. It was Richard Harris. He said, "Hal, we've got you booked on TWA, flight so and so, leaving tomorrow morning." I couldn't believe my ears. It was impossible. But if Jimmy was ready to go, I had to do my best. My passport was already in order, so I called Arlyn Henry, who ran our musician's answering service, and explained the situation. She had to juggle the schedule and get me out of ten full days of sessions, but as always, Arlyn and her girls worked wonders and made all the neccessary rearrangements.

I was picked up by a limo and whisked to LAX, where TWA gave me the VIP treatment all the way. The flight to London was a long one, but I was so excited I couldn't sleep. I arrived about 6 in the morning, and while going through customs when I was stopped by an immigration officer. In a very proper British voice, he asked if I was Hal Blaine, the American drummer. When I answered yes, he asked for my autograph. It was the beginning of a great trip for me. Imagine being known by a cop in England! He then asked what I was doing in England and I told him I would be recording with Richard Harris. When he brought up the matter of a work permit I told him it was my first trip to England and I didn't know anything about work permits. "Well don't worry about a thing, Mr. Blaine," he said, and proceeded to stamp my passport so that I was covered for everything possible.

I was met by Richard's chauffeur, who took me to the Belgravia apartment that Richard kept in London. I was invited into the palatial flat by his maid, Maria, and given coffee and rolls. By 7:30 a.m. I was ready to head for the studio and get to work.

By 10 I had finished my fifth cup of coffee and was anxiously awaiting some instructions. A voice that shook the walls called out "Marrria!" She went running off with a glass and a bottle of Pimm's. Pimm's was Richard's "wake up" in those days; it looked like pink champagne.

A few minutes later, Richard Harris strode into the room wearing a terrycloth robe that opened all the way down to his navel. With his arm outstretched, he vigorously shook my hand while his manhood swung from side to side. Quite an introduction. He asked me about the flight and I told him that everything had been wonderful, especially meeting the immigration agent. "Funny, they don't treat me that well," he said.

We sat down at his massive dining room table and had a gigantic breakfast. Throughout the meal, I kept expecting to leave any minute for the studio. We ate in silence and then Richard popped the million-dollar question. "Hal, do you know any good musicians over here like yourself?" I couldn't believe what I was hearing. I said, "Yes, but I'm sure they're all booked in advance at the studios now." Then came the second million-dollar zinger. "That brings me to my next question: Do you know of any good studios over here?" I was floored. I said, "Richard, I was under the impression that we were going directly to a studio today to start working. Where's Jimmy?" "Oh, don't worry about that, mate. Jimmy's in the country writing now. We plan on entertaining you royally for the next ten days." This was Jimmy's way of giving me a vacation that I will never forget. He also presented me with a handmade, solid gold Swiss watch inscribed "Hal, take time to live." And live we did. We partied for ten days straight and then all went back to Hollywood and recorded *MacArthur Park* at Sound Recorders. I had the pleasure and the privilege of conducting the string section during the overdub rehearsals. The project ended up as one of the finest trilogies ever recorded, and one of the most exciting times in my career.

In 1969, I purchased a 1927 Rolls Royce convertible roadster. It was a beautiful and elegant machine that I bought as a hobby to fix up and have fun with. Jimmy loved the car and asked me if I would drive his bride-to-be and her father (the actor Barry Sullivan) to their wedding ceremony at Jimmy Messina's ranch up in the mountains of Ojai, California. It was sure to be a gala occasion, and I was pleased to play such an honored role. But the morning of the wedding a very strange thing happened. Because it happened on the day of Jimmy's wedding it left an indelible impression. And because the guilty party, a very well-known record executive, has already paid the price for his wrongdoing, I won't drag him through it again here.

About 8:00 in the morning my son David, who was only 5 years old, came to my bedroom and said, "Dad, there are two men at the door to see you." I threw on my bathrobe and went to the door to find two guys flashing their FBI badges. "Get rid of the kid." they told me abruptly. I sent David to his room and stood there petrified. I couldn't understand why they were there. I had been paying all my taxes and had never had any run-ins with the law.

We entered my small office and one of the agents closed the

door behind him. "What's this all about?" I asked, still shaken up. One of them asked me, "Do you ever work for (a major record company)?" "Yes," I answered as they glanced around at the gold records and photos on the walls. "Just how do they pay you?" the other agent asked. I explained that when I worked at the studios we filled out W-4 forms, and then the company sent the checks to the musicians' union, where we picked them up and paid our work dues. All of the federal and state withholding taxes were automatically taken out. "Listen, every penny I earn is declared. I'm no cheater. My business manager takes care of all my taxes." I said.

"Do you ever get paid in cash?"

"No," I told them. "Never. It's always through a union contract."

One of the agents picked through his briefcase, pulled out a slip of paper and asked, "Did you work for (that company) on March 6, 7 and 8 of 1972?" I pulled out my ledger where I had recorded every date and every penny that I had ever received since starting in the studios. I flipped through the record and there it was: March 6,7,8; (the record company), NARM Show (National Association of Record Manufacturers); Miami, Florida; paid: $500 cash.

"Yes, you're right – here it is," I told them. "But I'm telling you this was declared on my taxes that year. My manager has all the records!" I was still shaking. "Mr. Blaine, we're not here to investigate you. We're here for another matter." They questioned me about the show, and I explained that the bandleader had hired me to go to Miami with his orchestra and singers. We performed as the house band along with featured artists from the label for the NARM audience. It was a very big annual affair.

"And just how did you physically get the money into your hands?" I explained that after the show we all lined up at the cashier's office and were taken in one by one and paid the cash. I received five one-hundred dollar bills. I remembered it well.

"And did you have to sign a receipt for the money?" "Yes, I did." With that, the agent then pulled another slip of paper out of his briefcase and asked me to look at it. It was a photostat, and with his hand over the top of the piece of paper, he asked, "Is this your signature?"

I answered, "Yes, sir:'

"And who handed you the five hundred?"

"It was a tall, bald-headed man. I forget his name, but he was in charge of paying everyone, I guess. I was first in line and there must have been 25 people behind me." The agent then removed his hand from the cash-paid slip and it read $1,000.

"Hold it, pal," I said. "I never got that thousand. I told you I got five hundred."

"We know. That's why we're here." Then the other agent reached into his briefcase and pulled out some photos and asked me if any of the men pictured had paid me. I immediately pointed to the picture of the bald-headed man. The agent then started reading the subpoena that had been prepared for me.

"The State of New Jersey hereby subpoenas you as a state's witness in the case of the State of New Jersey versus. . . You will appear on..."

"This isn't fair. I can't go to court in New Jersey;' I told them. "I'm booked solid for months in the studios!"

"No problem, Mr. Blaine. If we can use your typewriter, we'll take your statement right here and that'll be the end of it." They swore me in, typed out my statement and I signed it. I bid the gentlemen good-bye.

It was a terrifying experience to begin such a beautiful day, but I was relieved to be done with it. I got dressed, climbed into the Rolls and headed out to Jimmy's wedding.

13

The Mamas & The Papas– The World Learns About California Dreamin'

In the early '60s I was introduced to Lou Adler, one of the all-time great producers. A partner with Herb Alpert in some small productions during the early years, he was really starting to make a name for himself. Lou was a bright, clean-cut, good-looking guy – and quite a dresser. He was married at the time to Shelley Fabares and lived in a beautiful home in Bel-Air, the poshest neighborhood in the Hollywood scene.

I used to call Lou "the butcher boy," because I heard he was the son of a butcher from Boyle Heights. He had a great sense of humor, and we never started a session without swapping a half-dozen gags. He loved to enjoy himself and make good records.

Lou hired me while he was producing Shelley and Ann-Margret. (His credits read like a Who's Who of the recording world. Lou, Snuff Garrett, and Jimmy Bowen must hold some records for producing the most artists.) He was in charge of Trousdale Music and was well respected by The Wrecking Crew and by all of the studio personnel.

During his stint at Trousdale he formed Dunhill Records with Jay Lasker (the big cigar), who was running the Vee Jay Records operation. Almost overnight, Dunhill became very popular and ABC purchased it. It was renamed ABC Dunhill, a major label in a major market.

Lou had the Midas touch at Dunhill; everything he touched turned to gold. We were cutting records for Barry McGuire (*Eve of Destruction*,) Scott McKenzie (*San Francisco-Wear Some Flowers in Your Hair*,) Peter Allen, Gladys Knight & the Pips, Johnny Rivers, Barry Mann, P. F. Sloan, The Turtles, Carole King, and on and on. Lou loved to work, and work we did.

One quiet afternoon in December, 1965, he walked into the studio with a group he had just signed. Lou wanted Joe Osborn, Larry Knechtel and me to back up this non-playing group of singers from the East Coast. The four of them had been living on credit cards for some months in Jamaica and had moved on when the bills started catching up. The Mamas & the Papas were a strange group to look at – funny hats, old clothes from thrift stores and lots of antique jewelry. It was a motley crew, even by our Levi's standards.

Lou introduced us to the tall, bearded John Phillips and his beautiful, demure wife Michelle, the lanky, handsome Canadian, Denny Doherty, and the short and abundant Cass Elliot. John pulled out his guitar and started playing. They all joined in with *California Dreamin'*. Boy, could they sing! It was like a visit from angels. We couldn't believe the sweet, breathtaking harmony.

Their first album cover was outrageous. It pictured them in a bathtub and was called: *If You Can Believe Your Eyes and Ears – The Mamas & the Papas*. The cover proved to be an early force in creating the whole '60s trend for old clothing and a general dishevelment among teenagers.

John, a New York native, was quite a gifted songwriter. He was easy to get along with, but did have his temper tantrums now and then, mostly as a result of too much booze and cocaine. Songwriters sometimes forget that they know the songs backwards and forwards. They write it, they nurture it and they know it in their bones. I didn't, so I always insisted on a drum part as a guide. With John it was an absolute necessity. I've written out drum parts for every song I've ever recorded – that's how I always knew exactly what to do. Considering I was recording from five to 25 songs a day, you can understand why I liked to have a chart in front of me.

John tended to get lost by the time 4 a.m. rolled around. After he finished off a couple bottles of Chivas, I had to update him, reminding him of the current changes in the arrangement. He always asked me to get rid of the charts, but I knew better.

During one early morning session, the shit finally hit the fan. John had been making changes all night on a song and he couldn't remember them all. The tension was building. In the middle of the long-awaited take, he blew a 2/4 bar and blamed it on me.

"There – that was your goof, Blaine. Don't try to blame me for that one. I finally gotcha!"

That was all I had to hear. I couldn't take it any more. I blew my top, called him a lot of choice names and let him know what I thought of his guitar playing. The battle was on. Lou had to run into the studio to break it up. It had been a long day and we were all dog tired. I was sober as a judge, but John was plastered and his guitar playing just wasn't cutting it.

John and Lou took a walk, and John came back a little later with a quiet apology. I excused myself for getting carried away and we never had another outbreak.

Michelle was a striking, long-haired blonde from Hemet, California. She had a great voice, was always very quiet on the dates, but loved to laugh – like Lou. We had a lot of fun the night I gave her some Turkish bells to play on an overdub for Scott McKenzie's *San Francisco.* She did a good job and had a great time doing it.

After their album came out, the group had bookings all over the country. One of the first, a big Anaheim Stadium sell-out, turned into a total disaster. The Mamas & the Papas were being introduced and Michelle was missing. John ran around like a madman and finally found her calmly talking with a musician from another group in the backstage lounge.

That was it. He was nervous and furious enough to fire her on the spot. She did go on, but it was her last appearance with the group for a while. She was replaced by Jill Stewart, then the girlfriend of Jan Berry. Jill had Michelle's looks, but she couldn't pull off that unique singing style. Things cooled off, and before long John and Michelle patched things up. The Mamas & the Papas were back together again.

Denny Doherty was a pussycat. As a good-looking bachelor, he became a '60s heartthrob and had the girls screaming in the aisles. A quiet Canadian, Denny also liked his Chivas and was never without it. Everyone got along well with Denny. He had a quiet sense of humor and wasn't the kind of person to make waves.

Mama Cass was a Jewish girl from New York and I've never met a sharper lady, with the possible exception of Barbra Streisand. Cass had that built-in Manhattan savvy and the streetwise sass of a hooker. She was very intelligent and seemed to be the only levelheaded one in the group. Cass was simply a chubby, wonderful gal that loved to sing and dress up in bizarre outfits that hung from her body like tents. Each time we met at the studio she appeared in more oudandish outfits.

The group was going nuts with the money. John and Michelle bought the old Jeanette McDonald mansion in Bel-Air, not far from Lou Adler's place. Denny bought the Mary Astor mansion in Beverly

Hills and Cass bought a beautiful spread up in the Hollywood Hills. John would call Lou and say, "Let's go out to lunch – what'll it be, Rolls Royces or Jeeps?" They were all buying new cars, expensive toys and having a great time with the wealth and stardom. Before long we noticed a change in Lou. He grew a beard, started wearing weird clothes and began to look more like The Mamas & the Papas than the kids themselves.

Some of the wilder incidents took place in the attic studio that John built in the famous McDonald mansion. It was strictly illegal to have a home studio in Bel-Air, but he did it anyway. As you walked up the grand staircase to the bedrooms, you could push one of the mahogany panels that lined the walls and a door opened, revealing a hidden staircase up to the studio. All of the heavy duty power came through the basement and the wiring was concealed throughout the house. The studio was completely soundproofed by the best designers and builders in town.

This was a swank neighborhood (across the street was the famous Kirkeby mansion, the one used for The Beverly Hillbillies TV show), and it became routine for the Bel-Air police to drop by while we were recording to check out all the cars and trucks in the driveway. When the cops arrived, we'd all rush down from the studio into the den where instruments were set up. In the middle of a "rehearsal" the police would be invited in and told, "Well of course we're making music here – we're The Mamas & the Papas." They'd go away scratching their heads, knowing something was fishy, but they never discovered the secret studio.

The equipment in the studio was the same gear that the kids had recorded all of their hits on. Western Studios had sold them the entire contents of Studio Three.

John had all these personal recording toys to play with and Lou was inspired to pursue a new career: He wanted to learn how to be an engineer. Peter Pilafian usually did all of the engineering for John, but when he wasn't around Lou took over the controls. We'd be working in the middle of the night and Lou would say, "Let's make it!" and we would. Then he would try to play it back and find that the tape was blank. When it happened more than once, I nicknamed him "F-Troop."

If you have some of the early albums, you'll see credits that read: "Engineered by F-Troop:' It was great making records in that house. I wasn't into grass, but we were all treated like royalty and there was always a smorgasbord of consumables for everyone. And there was something special about those illicit sessions that gave us all a thrill.

But every party ends. The Mamas &: the Papas finally called it quits. John and Michelle divorced, sold the estate and took off in different directions. She started showing up in films and began a new career as an actress.

Denny's luck began to sour. He lost his Beverly Hills home, became a hard-core alcoholic and was practically living on skid row in Florida. It got so bad that he ended up jumping out of a second story window and breaking both his legs. When it made the news, Lou found Denny and took him under his wing. He got him the best medical treatment that money could buy and set him up with a new recording contract. Denny stopped drinking, and after his stay in the hospital we got together for a record that turned out to be a fine piece of work. We were all grateful that Lou saved Denny from total self-destruction.

The solo records we did with Cass were all hits, including my favorite, *Dream a Little Dream of Me*. She dropped the "Mama" image and became a star in her own right – Cass Elliot. She was doing great, singing her songs and appearing on all the top shows. The world was looking very bright for Cass when it all suddenly ended. She died of heart failure in her London hotel suite. It was devastating for all of us and officially ended an era of California Dreamin'.

14

The Carpenters

Way back in the good ol' days of 1969-1970, Joe Osborn and I were inseperable in the studios, working every conceivable type of date imaginable. It was during this period that Joe mentioned that he had been recording an interesting group in his garage studio. He kept touting these kids as a fresh and up and coming group that would certainly hit the big time in the near future.

Joe kept asking me to think about producing these kids. For awhile, I had been producing some nondescript acts to no avail. Good recordings with a series of personal and management problems that kept some great records off the charts. Joe, Larry Knechtel, and I were doing a Neil Diamond date at Sound Recorders when Joe asked me to come outside during a break and meet some people. It was the Carpenters.

I was introduced to two sort of chubby kids that seemed to be in their tens. Richard was a nice looking young man dressed in semi-western garb and Karen wore a leather fringed western jacket. They were both on cloud nine just being outside of the studio where Neil was recording.

Karen and Richard both had a rather strange lisp when they spoke, not at all bad, but quite noticeable. I figured it was probably caused by having worn dental braces as children. The meeting was brief and called short when Armin Steiner soon burst out of the front door and said that Neil was ready to go back to work. I shook hands with the kids and we said our goodbyes.

Later that night after work, Joe and I sat down to discuss these teenagers. "Joe, I'm sure they're great kids, but an organ player and a girl drummer? It doesn't make sense. Who the hell will want them? They're not country and they're not rock. And besides, where the hell are we gonna find the time to really do a good job with them?" Joe agreed, and that was that. Talk about losing a gold mine. Well, it wouldn't be my first time.

The Carpenters weren't heard of again for some time, and then, what a surprise – I happened to hear their first recording, on the A&M label. They'd been signed, and I was really happy for them and for Joe, who played bass. Unfortunately, nothing happened with their first couple of records, and then I got a call from Jack Daugherty, the great trumpet player and producer. He wanted me and Joe to come in and make some Carpenter records. We did, and of course, the rest is history. *We've Only Just Begun*, which was also the famous Paul Williams, Roger Nichols commercial for Crocker Bank, was now climbing the charts.

In the studio, the kids were great. Karen sang her pretty buns off and Richard was wonderful on the piano. He was one of the most prolific arrangers I had ever worked with.

We were recording constantly and it was hit after hit with these teenagers from Downey, California. They became the golden geese, laying all the golden eggs for A&M. Herb Alpert and Jerry Moss, my old partners in crime, couldn't have been happier. I, of course, was kicking my butt all the way home after each session, knowing that I was the boob who turned down the Carpenters.

After a few smash hits, Karen came to me and asked me to have a drum kit made exactly like mine so she could play the same arrangements on the road. I had been using my monster Octaplus custom drums on all of their records. I very diplomatically asked, "When the hell are you gonna stop playing the drums and start fronting this outfit?" For some reason, to me, women seemed to look rather awkward playing a set of drums. Don't get me wrong, she was a great drummer, but just had a sort of strange look sitting at the drums.

I obviously said the wrong thing, because Jack and Richard jumped on me. "Don't make waves," I was told very nicely. That's the way the folks want it, and that's that.

The senior Carpenters were pretty upset at me in the beginning because they felt that Karen should be playing on the records. I was told that Mrs. Carpenter said, "I've seen many drummers on TV and Karen is as good as any of them." She didn't understand the technical side of recording, and she was, of course, trying to protect her daughter, the drummer. But only the drummer. Richard was the star of the show, but not for long, I guess.

Howie Oliver built her a set of drums and she was very pleased. Richard and Karen had now been around the country on promo tours, personal appearances, and were really in the big time. They both lost their baby fat and looked great. They started buying beautiful jewelry and cars, and were quickly becoming part of the Hollywood gang. Their records went Number One, and they were feted wherever they appeared or went. Fan magazines, Billboard, Cash Box, and all of the industry trades were hailing them as the new super group, and they were.

Well, after so many hits and so many bucks, The Carpenters chose to start making their own records. As is the case with so many groups, historically speaking, this is usually the beginning of the end. "Why should we spend so much on producers and musicians when we can do it ourselves?" They continued to do personals and they did their own records, but it seemed like the Top Ten was now out of their reach. In retrospect, I guess you could say that they had had their run. They were always working, Richard's arrangements were still magnificant, and Karen was singing better than ever. They had really matured as musicians and entrepreneurs, with Karen in front of the band and Richard playing and conducting. They hired a fine drummer and all seemed pretty smooth to most of us.

I would see Karen from time to time in the studio when I was working with The Captain and Tenille or some other A&M group. We were always as friendly as day one, but I did notice that when I was hugging her, I could feel her rib cage from behind and she was getting thinner all the time. I wasn't in on the home scene, but rumor had it that she had finally met the man of her dreams. But he soon took her for a bundle and ran off. That was the rumor, mind you. Karen seemed to be disintegrating before everyone's eyes. We didn't know about her anorexic condition, a very hard disease to overcome. She passed away so young and so vital. But I'll always remember her as that kid from Downey in the fringed jacket.

Years later, Richard called me in to do some updating on some of the older tracks and I worked about five or six hours, crying all the way, and I wasn't the only one. We all had a good cry that day, but I'm sure that Karen was smiling down on us from up there, with the Mona Lisa smile of hers. I was thinking of this after Nat King Cole's death when Capital Records had me come in and add drums to many of his tracks, and one of the songs was *Mona Lisa*.

Carpenters' Hit List, not including Album Cuts
Hal Blaine, drums

1970
We've Only Just Begun
Close To You

1971
I Won't Last A Day Without You
Rainy Days And Mondays
Superstar
For All We Knew
Sebastian
The Road Ode
What Are You Doing For Love?
Bless The Beasts And The Children

1972
Goodbye To Love
I Believe In You

1973
Top Of The World
Yesterday Once More

1974
Jambalaya

15

The John Denver Story

On October 29, 1970, I walked into Studio C at A&M and recorded a commercial for Northwest National Bank with a relatively unknown folk singer. I had no idea that less than four years later I would be a part of his group, riding the charts week after week and performing for millions of fans.

On a weekly basis I was doing shows like *Happy Days* and *Alias Smith & Jones*, commercials for sponsors like Coca-Cola, Goodyear, Mazda and Budweiser, and films such as *The Harrod Affair, Walking Tall* and *Jonathan Livingston Seagull*. I was recording with Johnny Mathis, David Cassidy & The Partridge Family, Dean Martin, Barbra Streisand, and on and on. I had become a household word in just about every studio from Burbank to Culver City and.was feeling pretty comfortable. I had a beautiful home. My children, David and Michelle, now six and eight years old, were enrolled in the best private schools.We spent many happy vacations together, sometimes flying to places like Hawaii for a week or two – not a bad existence.

When John Denver's producer, Milt Okun, called four years after the commercial date and asked me to record with John, I was flattered that John had remembered me. He was doing his first West Coast album, *Back Home Again*, and it was a dream job. John had grown from a young folkie to a fully blossomed pop singer. He had a special honesty that came across in his songs. It was simply down home, everyone's dream of a happy life. Everyone around John shared the dream and the good feeling radiated everywhere. At the close of his shows, it was common for the audience to stand and start chanting "John Denver for President."

Kris O'Connor was road managing and co-producing. John Sommers was playing fiddle, picking banjo and singing backgrounds.

(Later, he would write *Thank God I'm a Country Boy* for John.) Steve Weisberg was on rhythm and steel guitar. He was a tall, handsome Texan who sang with a slight lisp that the ladies loved. Dick Kniss, a New Yorker by way of Portland, Oregon, who had toured for years with Peter, Paul and Mary, was on bass.

The first song I recorded with John was *Back Home Again,* although the credits were mistakenly given to Jimmy Gordon. When we finished the album, John asked me to play some percussion goodies with him for a concert or two. I'd had similar offers from other artists, but when I told them how busy I was and how much money I'd need to miss work in Hollywood, I usually didn't hear from them until they were ready to record again. John was different, and I was soon headed for St. Paul to augment the John Denver band.

John was a true gentleman and was always considerate of his musicians. It was first-class all the way, and it was a great way to get spoiled.

I brought along a set of congas, some assorted shakers and wind chimes, a cymbal tree and some extra cymbals. The dates came off without a hitch. When we finished, John told me that my contribution was exactly what had been missing – no drums, just effects. "Will ya do some more concerts with me, Hal?" he asked. I said yes, and John hugged me and welcomed me to the band.

Before long I really felt like a part of the group. My opinions were asked and treated with respect. I was the old man of the group and knew my way around the world of show business. My ideas were usually valid and helped the shows in one way or another.

Aside from all the gold records I had worked on, I had done more than my share of concerts, and I was just passing my knowledge on to John and the group. He was grateful, and the group was glad to have me as a permanent member. We got along as close friends, and the weekends turned into short tours lasting two or three weeks. I loved every minute of it.

I learned to relax with John and feel good about myself. I learned more about respect and family than I had ever known in the past. John's wife Annie was an absolute dream girl. She had been his only love since their college days and was his inspiration from their first date. They both had wonderful families, and it was a pleasure to be around these simple, elegant people with their country roots.

1975 was quite a year for me with John Denver. In my first year on the road I played more one-nighters than I had done in my entire career. We criss-crossed the country from Los Angeles to New

York and played all the cities in between. We had a crew of 75 taking care of all the backstage work. Everyone from bus drivers to baggage handlers shared in the happiness instilled by John, and we all had a great time being with such a hit show.

During one of our Saturday morning rehearsals in a San Fernando Valley studio, I met my wife-to-be (wife number five.) My buddy Rick Verdi had been telling me about a "wonderful" girl who would be perfect for me. When we met, she was wearing old Army clothing (she had been an Army nurse), bundled to the neck, and sported an old hat that just showed a curl of blonde hair. I got her number and told her I'd call, but she seemed uninterested, so I decided to pass. Rick wouldn't give up though. He kept after me, and we finally arranged to have a date.

When I walked through the door, I knew I was looking at the woman of my dreams. She was a 6-foot blonde from Texas who looked like a movie star, with silver blonde hair down to her shoulders and a smile that could melt an iceberg. She'd been an Air Force brat and was specializing in intensive care nursing at the UCLA Medical Center. I was ready for marriage, although I'd been single for four years, swearing never to marry again. Here in front of me stood my next six years, nine months and 12 hours of wedded bliss. We were married four months later, in June 1975.

Just before our marriage, my fiancee called her mother in Abilene, Texas, and told her to watch the John Denver special. She told her mom, "When you see the drummer, take a good look – he'll soon be your son-in-law." Of course, all the family gathered around the TV to see the new relation. Unfortunately, my fiancee had forgotten to mention that I was playing percussion, not drums. Herb Lavelle, a fine looking black man, was on drums for the concert. During the show, the camera zoomed right into the audience for a full-face close-up of my fiancee, and then faded to a commercial. I'm sure John arranged it.

The next shot after the commercial was of Herb Lavelle drumming with his sticks on a board. It was a country scene, and we were all dressed for the parts. I was playing washboard and Danny Kaye was the special guest. When the show was over, my fiancee called home to see what the family thought. They were paralyzed. Her mother, a real Texan, said, "I guess you know what you're doing, but it'll be a tough life being married to a black man." John and Annie arranged for our wedding to take place on the top of a mountain in Aspen. The entire band was there with their families. John was best man, Annie was matron of honor, and Kris and Bonnie O'Connor's kids were flower children. We all wore the floral arrangements that Annie designed for our hair. John sang *Annie's Song*, and the day couldn't have been more beautiful The reception was held at John's house high in the mountains, and everyone drank champagne and partied. We then gathered for a special dinner at one of John's favorite restaurants.

John took me aside at one point during the reception and, like a father, kissed me on the cheek and said, "Hal, you're not going to be pounding those drums all of your life. When you and your bride are ready to take it easy, come up here and settle down." He pointed out of his picture window and said, "Pick out anything you like – it's yours." The first six years of my marriage brought perfect domestic happiness. My wife accepted the grind of my work routine and was a gracious hostess with our friends. Everyone fell in love with her. My family adored her. This was the marriage I had been waiting for all of my life.

The show was scheduled to travel to England at one point, and at the last minute Herb Lavelle had to cancel. Kris O'Connor called me and asked if I could possibly play drums as well as percussion. "Hell, yes!" I replied. I had studied independent coordination for so long I sometimes felt like I was schizophrenic. From that day on, I played the sit-down set and the percussion for John.

John's traveling procedure was one of the best I've ever seen with bands, thanks to our do-everything travel planner, John Clark. We always left L.A. in the morning, arrived in the East that afternoon, and spent the first night resting. The flights were always fun and well-planned, and we were able to relax and eat like kings. John called it a sharkfest and later called us the sharks. "Johnny and The Sharks" stuck for a long time.

We generally took over the entire top floor of the hotels we stayed at and had a security officer at the elevator. No one could get off on our floor without the special John Denver Show badge. We also had our own security force led by John's personal security man, Tom Crum, an incredible martial arts instructor from John's Windstar Foundation in Snowmass, Colorado.

The next day we started work for real, if you could call it work. We usually left for the venue at 4 p.m., giving us almost an entire day to sight-see: shop, make calls, etc. The soundcheck came off about 5 and we finished by 6 or 6:30. As the concert hall doors opened, we would go off to our well-stocked dressing rooms for rest and relaxation. John had a ping-pong table backstage at each hall, and the ping-pong wars would rage as the audience was being seated for the 8 o'clock show. Most of the cast and crew were avid ping-pongers, but none of them had the killer instinct like John. No one could beat him except Lowell Norman, and he only did it every once in a great while.

John always saw to it that the handicapped were allowed into the auditorium first and given the best seats in the house. It did my heart good to see some of these folks at ringside clapping and cheering from their wheelchairs. At the end of each show I would jump off the stage and hand my sticks to one of them. It broke my heart more than once, but it made them feel so good.

At the end of each show, a special backstage section was set up for visiting dignitaries, mayors, governors and presidential families. Record distributors, RCA officials, agents and disc jockeys, and any and all friends of the band were invited. We always had carte blanche as to how many complimentary seats we wanted, and in Texas one night, I had about 15 of the family in. Los Angeles was the only exception, where we were given a limited number of complimentary seats. L.A. was, of course, a madhouse when we played, and the audience was filled with friends of the business, friends of John's personal manager Jerry Weintraub, as well as film stars, producers, directors, etc.

If, on occasion, we had to do two shows on the same evening, there was a catered, sit-down dinner served to everyone connected with the show. But generally, we only did one show, and after the dignitary get-together, we would head for the airplane, hop aboard for another sharkfest and fly on to the next date to do it all again.

But times change and people change. Sometimes an outside event can change people's lives. In this case, it was Elvis Presley. When Elvis died, John decided to revamp the band. John Sommers had quit; Steve Weisberg quit after a painful divorce; and Dick Kniss and his wife started a business in New York. To fill out the band, we hired James Burton on guitar, Glen D. Hardin on piano and Emory Gordy on Fender bass– all Presley alumni. Herb Pederson was brought in on banjo and guitar, Danny Weetman on fiddle, Jim Horn on sax and flute, and away we went. It was a terrific band with tremendous energy onstage. John was playing all kinds of guitars and starting to rock.

I think this was the beginning of the end. The fans loved John for the things he did naturally, the style that set him apart. Although we had a great band, we started sounding more like other pop bands. The special John Denver quality seemed to change, and the fans couldn't identify with him like before.

The new band wanted John to rock more, while the fans wanted *Annie's Song* and the other classics. John used to come to me and say, "Hal, if you see me going too far over to the rock side, grab me and straighten me out." I tried on several occasions, but John had that electric guitar bit clenched in his teeth and there was no stopping him. His marriage began to crumble, along with his popularity.

Although I didn't realize it at the time, I was about to play my final inning with the John Denver Show. In retrospect, it was comical as well as very sad and disillusioning. We were heading for a tour of Japan. I had requested a sleeper (paid for by me) because I had worked late the night before, and this was going to be a long flight. When we boarded the plane, my berth was taken by one of the brass in our party. At the last minute, some of the management people decided to take the same flight, so I was bumped. I was exhausted, but I was booked first class and stretched out there.

When we arrived in Japan, John sent down orders that we were to meet at a certain hour to play baseball with the Tokyo Giants at their stadium. I always acted as the announcer during our games, doing my microphone shtick, prodding the guys on, but this time I just couldn't make it. I was totally wasted from the trip. John felt that my action was a slap in the face to the Japanese fans. I felt bad, because I would never have hurt their feelings intentionally.

Then we did two TV shows from a major TV studio. Since they were nationally advertised specials for Japan, I suggested that we get paid scale for the shows. It was just a few bucks, and it wasn't money out of John's pocket, because the shows were sponsored by JVC (Japanese Victor Company) and NEC (Nippon Electric Company), the corporate equivalents to General Electric in America. I only was asking for what was rightfully ours. The band agreed, but no one backed me up. I was going over the top alone, rifle in hand, facing the fully armed enemy: the Denver managers. I really didn't mean to upset anyone; this wasn't a labor strike. But it didn't go over very well.

The next bit of friction went back a little farther, but I bring it out now because this is where it fits into the picture. Not long before leaving for Japan we lost Emory Gordy, our beloved bass player, and then the scramble was on to find a replacement. Every guy in the band wanted their own man, and every time a bass player came out for a try, the majority would rule. Eventually, a player was chosen. He was a nice guy, but he came from a hard-rock group and had no musical finesse whatsoever.

We tried doing an album, but this new guy couldn't even keep a simple time beat going. It was ludicrous. The album just wasn't happening. We had all lost that lovin' feeling, and I was really hurt when I heard that certain band members had voted to toss me out because the bass player said he couldn't play with me. Fortunately, John vetoed the idea, realizing that my expertise was in recording and the fault wasn't mine. The album was scrapped, and John went to Nashville and recorded with some Nashville cats.

Back to Japan. When we arrived at the TV studio for the show, a new gofer/valet/aspiring-to-producer asked us to listen to John's new album. We all listened and thought it was fine. No big noisemaker, but a nice album. As for the drum parts, they were fine, but for Nashville, it sounded pretty busy. Nashville was just discovering the percussion sounds that most of us on the West Coast were shelving from overuse. John's album was loaded with clicks, bangs, dings and pops at practically every song opening. It sounded a bit silly, but I kept my mouth shut.

Mr. Gofer asked me to particularly listen to the bass drum sound. The band all listened and when the record finished, I said, "What about it?" He said, "This is the sound that we want to get from now on." I said, "That is the exact sound that's coming from my bass drum."

The Denver set that I used on the road was loaded with foam rubber. It had a perfect recording sound with the head off in the studio, but on the road I had a head on the front featuring John's Windstar logo. The American Indian motif was part of the Denver stage set, designed by John's company, Goshe Graphics. It looked and sounded beautiful.

The gofer persisted: "Well, the drummer in Nashville didn't have a head on the front of his drum, and that's what I want!" Now the band was looking at me, holding back their laughter. I couldn't help but laugh, and it pissed him off. "Go ahead and laugh, but I want that head off of there for this tour." "Okay," I said, "but what about all of those funny little things that are holding the head on? How about all of those little things rattling at once? That oughta sound great!"

Now the band was near hysterics, and the argument was getting hot. I looked at Steve Voudouris, our head roadie, and said, "Take it off." John appeared and tried to stop the silliness, but the want-to-be manager really had to show his stuff. "That's right, Steve, take it off!" shouted the gofer. I said, "Look, if you had ever taken the time to look at my sets – and there are nine of them – you'd have noticed that none of them have a head on the front. I haven't used front heads for years in the studios." Then the gofer said, "Well, don't think I don't know something about music – I used to play trumpet in high school!" I looked at the band and said, "I rest my case." The band rolled in the aisles.

After the fiascos of the Japanese tour, John went to China for some R&R. He had studied Buddhism and was getting in tune with the old religious scene there. One day I received a wonderful post-card from China. That very night I got a call from the gofer: "Hal, we won't be needing you on the show anymore. We're hiring the Nashville drummer." Click.

The end had come. The gofer had scored. I was heartbroken to say the least and, to top it all off, a few weeks later my wife ran off. Within a year, John's wife filed for divorce.

About a year later, John sent me the nicest trophy in my collection – a gold record to end all gold records. It was a goldframed, nine gold-record set of all the albums that I did with John. And, although I did lose to the gofer, I still think that somehow, down deep, John knew that I was as loyal to him as a person could be. I think that I was the winner.

16

Married To My Drums

My drums have always been my closest friends. I love playing alone or with others. This was my way of communicating in the world; the music world was the only one I seemed to have any regard for. I was terrible in school, but I was wonderful in "drums." Maybe it was the showoff syndrome, but as a kid I always felt I would become a start and buy my parents a home and anything my brothers and sisters ever wanted. We were so damn poor. All I knew was that music was to be my lifelong profession. There was really nothing else.

If there is one thing I want to pass on to the up-and-comers in the music world, it's the fact that to be truly successful you must become married to your instrument. You may wed a wonderful person, but it takes someone special to understand that they will always play "second chair" to your musical instrument. This probably holds true for other instruments, too, whether it's a scalpel or a monkey wrench. The second thing is to find a balance between you, your instrument and your family. Balance is everything. If you spend your life practicing, playing, eating, and sleeping music, you will probably end up a mental case.

It's also essential to be a good listener. Music is a collaborative art form. You must always be aware of what the others are playing because you use their efforts in building a song, a riff, or an arrangement.

As a kid, drumming was my entire life. My sister Marcia bought my first drum kit when I was 13, and I've worked day and night ever since, pounding out my life. I was tormented with school and the poverty of my daily life, but in my private musical world I experienced the greatest natural high a person could feel. This is probably why I never got into the heavy drinking and drugs that seem to be a part of growing up these days. Of course, drugs were not a part of growing up in a ghetto in the '30s. It wasn't until the headlines broke "Gene Krupa, Dope Fiend, Jailed" that marijuana became a common item in the papers and also became associated with music.

After long years of paying my dues in cheap clubs from coast to coast and developing my chops, I made it to Hollywood and started building a reputation as a session drummer. At first, I was like any other drummer. I had my drums in the car, I'd go to the gig, sweat it out setting up, then sit down and try to be comfortable and creative. It was an exhausting grind.

I realized I had to make some changes if I wanted to accelerate my career and succeed. Hollywood had the solution ready and waiting for me: cartage. The cartage company delivered my drums, and arriving at the studio a half-hour early, I set them up, played the date, packed up the drums, and the cartage company picked them up. It was wonderful – well, almost.

Half the time my drums were delivered to the wrong studio. Other times a case or two would be missing, and I would panic to get things ready in time. Sometimes they were left at the front door of the studio, and I would have to haul them through the maze of cables and microphone stands that had been set up. When my session calls started multiplying, I added a second set of drums to make scheduling easier. The record companies paid the cartage bill, which was $4.25 a session when I started. (My last cartage bill was $165. Times have changed, but butter used to be a nickel a pound when I was a kid.)

I was so busy I found it impossible to handle setting up and playing all the dates I was called for. There was only one solution. I needed a roadie, someone to set up and tear down and haul the sets of drums from studio to studio. The guy I found was Rick Faucher, a young kid who was working for Wally Heider on remote recording dates. He was a natural: a music fan and a mechanical genius. Rick built race cars as a hobby, and he straightened out my cars more than once when I had trouble.

Rick lived just off the Hollywood Freeway, minutes from all the top studios. It took me 25 years to develop my own setup, but I taught it to him in one day. I could call him at the last minute, and he'd have my drums at the studio and set up in minutes.

When I first notified the cartage company that I would no longer be using their service, the shit hit the fan. They told me I couldn't get my drums out of storage, because there was a few hundred bucks in past-due bills from some of the record companies. They had a California Public Utilities Commission license, and no one could deliver without that license. The word got back to me that I had better not mess with these people. They were known as arm and leg-breakers and had some pretty shady connections.

I was badly shaken by the situation, but I also had a few friends who were known as tough characters. I talked things out with my business manager, Phil Singer, and we hit on a plan. Phil met with the district attorney, and we found out that I could legally get around the cartage companies and the Teamsters if I had a personal valet. So Rick officially became my valet (and knew he was taking a risk in doing so). We had a letter sent out to all the cartage companies from the DA stating that if anything happened to me, Rick, or our families, a formal investigation would be conducted. We were making a major change in the way the music business ran in Hollywood.

I paid off the old cartage bills, got my drums and Rick took over. Then the cartage companies started taking movies of Rick delivering my drums. He was subject to continual harassment, but this skinny kid, who weighed about 105 soaking wet, never flinched. They made life difficult, but they never laid a finger on him, me or my drums. I was still holding my special police officer's rating from the San Bernardino Police Department and a concealed weapons permit, and I was never without my .38 detective special.

Within a couple of months, Rick was setting me up four or five times a day. On the weekends he kept the equipment in top order. I soon had five kits, and Rick hired some of his friends to keep them all in perfect condition. He would change heads as necessary, or follow instructions on notes I left after a session. He even drove to dates in San Francisco, San Diego and Las Vegas. He insisted that he maintain everything personally and had carte blanche at the pro drum shops, per my request.

Many record companies refused to honor my cartage bills for Rick. We were getting in the hole with all the bills, and my business manager came up with another solution: set Rick up with his own cartage company. He got his PUC license, a new Ford van and was in business. I was making quite a name for myself, and soon other drummers started calling Rick to handle their cartage, but he told them he was too busy working for me. Before long, many drummers wanted a personal setup man like I had.

The cartage companies were between a rock and a hard place. They came to Rick and offered him all kinds of bribes to work for them. He was a hot commodity, but he stuck by me. The next step was for the cartage companies to hire and train special drum-setup personnel. The rest is history. If nothing else, Hollywood drummers can thank Rick and me for breaking the ice. Today, a drummer can walk in and play a job as a gentleman. The union passed legislation that a company hiring a drummer/percussionist has to pay for cartage. That led to the same benefits for bass players, harpists and other musicians who had to haul a cumbersome instrument to a date. It also includes the elaborate electronic setups common these days.

Rick stuck with me throughout the golden Hollywood years. He eventually started handling Jim Keltner, Ringo Starr and Larry Brown, among others. Everyone in Hollywood knew Rick and respected him. He was one of the few guys who had keys to all the studios and alarm systems and could walk in at any time, day or night, for a setup. Rick was always giving a helping hand to the setup guys at the studios, and he was also never too busy to grab a sandwich for a musician.

Rick was instrumental in creating my monster drum kit, a development that changed the sound of recorded music and put me at the top of my profession. Through my requests and guidance, he worked closely with Howie Oliver and the Pro Drum Shop to make that first set with the elaborate tom racks, which we called Octoplus. Rick used to call me "The Naz," referring to Lord Buckley's characterization of Jesus. "The Naz never did nothing small," he would say.

The development of my monster drum set led to the kits that are marketed today by every drum company, including the electronic drum companies. I had no idea then of the impact my introduction of midrange tuning and the racks of drums would have, or that it would mean recording studios would have to invest in lots of microphones to handle the proliferation of big kits. Of course, sampling and synthesizers have brought more changes to the studios, but they'll never replace a live kit in performance. And today, after the newness of all these electronic devices has worn thin, we're seeing a return to some of the basic, good ol' drumming of the past. Looking back over the years, I feel proud and lucky to have been a small part of a great era of record making. I have my gold records and photos, and I can always turn on the radio and hear my drums on hits that will live on long after I'm gone.

17

Hal Blaine, 1990

When you come to the end of a book, the hero usually dies or lives happily ever after. In my case it's more of a slow fade into semi-retirement, along with some new beginnings.

As the synthesizers, drum machines, computers and high-tech recording styles of the '80s came rolling into the studios, I was called for fewer and fewer sessions. Time is money, and percussion shortcuts replaced traditions laid down over the years by me and other professionals. Just as my buddies and I had walked into the studios in the late '50s and taken over, it was now time for the younger players who had paid their dues to take control.

This new group, which had grown up with the new recording technology, was the perfect match for the music industry machine of the '80s-Hollywood meets Silicon Valley. The new musicians found computers to be very friendly, and while I've learned to peck away at my word processor, for the most part the computer is not my strong instrument.

I packed up and moved to Palm Springs. First-class shows come to town and I can sit in now and then. It's also close enough for the short commute to L.A. and some steady, slower-paced studio work. My children have grown up and are on their own. The homes, boats, cars, and motorcycles that were such a part of my life in Hollywood just don't mean as much anymore.

I was surprised by my first offer to go back on the road. It was with Mason Williams, my old *Classical Gas* pal from the '60s. Rick Cunha, Mason's studio partner, talked him into leaving his farm in Oregon for a tour combining his bluegrass group with symphony orchestras throughout the country. Working during the Pops concert season, our show is lively and action-packed, taking full advantage of Mason's great comedic writing talents. His gifts as a musician and humorist, developed while working on the Smothers Brothers' shows, have found a warm reception wherever we play.

Byron Berline is on fiddle, and the concert violinists are knocked out by his touch. John Hickman, on the five-string banjo, blows the classical musicians away with his speed and dexterity. Jerry Mills on mandolin is another speedster who loves to leave us in the dust, and his quick wit always comes at just the right time to ease the stage tension. Don Waley's wailin' Fender bass and high harmonies complete our hot ensemble. We play concert halls across the country, and it is a gas to be working again with such fine talents.

We are a pretty crusty-looking bunch of bluegrass boys, and the orchestras typically give us the snob brush-off at first. But after they become familiar with Mason's material and arrangements they join us on stage with hearty enthusiasm.

While we were out on the road, I got a call from David Grisman. He and his band had attracted quite a following for his special brand of bluegrass-oriented music, which he calls "Dawg Music." David told me he wanted to add drums and give it a new twist.

We recorded an album called *Acousticity*, and I was given a free hand to experiment with drums and percussion. It was great to be on an album project again, but I felt it might be my swan song, my last cruise before retirement. Shortly after the album's release, David called to tell me the album was doing well and he wanted me to go out on tour with the band.

Back on the road again. This time I was the oldest guy in the group. But I felt like a 10-year-old kid, traveling with David, John Sholle, Rob Wasserman, and Jim Buchanan. David's manager, Craig "Clag" Miller, was also our van driver. Clag was the utility genius on these excursions; arranging, producing, road managing, working with the sound and lights, and anything else that needed expert attention. It wasn't as hard as during my early touring days, but it took me back to those long drives on the road. The quality of the music was so fine– "in the pocket," as they say. Everyone was in tune, the timing was perfect and there were no fights about proper tempo. It was a far cry from my days of international touring with stars like John Denver, but it was good to be working and making good music again.

There's something special about playing the smaller circuits. There's an intimacy, the audiences are very attentive, and I'm always getting notes passed to me backstage from folks who know my work. The drummers in the small towns go out of their way to get in touch, and it's a nice feeling to be remembered and appreciated by fans and working musicians across the country.

I'm happy to say that I still get that rush of energy, and a fulfilling sensation comes over me when I go out onstage or into the studio for some recording. I recently did a session with Snuff Garrett and the old feelings were just as strong as ever. On the first tune, I immediately turned a few things around, did some rearranging and everybody loved it. I've always worked with a formula – look at the chart and block out the verses and the choruses and try to come up with some hooks. It just comes to me and, thank God, it still seems to be an important part of making records.

The hook has always been important to me – that repetitive sound that happens in the intro, after the first chorus, maybe just before the end. It's something that makes you take notice, a piece of the song that stands out by itself. My "bump ba bump bam" helped make that Phil Spector sound. My inspiration comes from what I feel, and I've always tried to work with the meaning in the lyrics.

These days, as I expected, the jobs are coming less and less frequently and I find myself with more time on my hands. I guess it's natural to start wondering about the meaning of all my years in this business, and what I might have done differently. It's nice to browse through my records and reflect on the happy times, but I realize how fast the ride at the top is and how important it is to plan for the future.

I've had ups and downs, as most musicians do in their careers. It gets different as you get older, though. There are the lean times, but they never seem lean when you're a kid and you're struggling and fighting and trying to make the car payments. It's tougher when you get older.

Some of the great stars I worked with were very appreciative of the contributions of the studio players, and others really didn't pay much attention. Royalties, bonuses, or long-range rewards weren't our concern, and that remains one of my greatest regrets. When we were hot, we were hot. After things cooled out, we all wished we had stashed away more than memories of the good times.

The music has sustained me, though. There were many nights as a kid when I was going through a bout of depression and I just got out the pad and sticks and started whooping it up and enjoying myself. I still do it.

It gets to me when I realize that my drums and my rhythms are being pumped out all over the world every day. Wherever I go, here in the States or overseas, I find people who know my work. I can't believe the fan mail I get from places I've never seen. I've touched strangers, people I will never meet from cultures I will never comprehend. The music has become a part of their lives. It's limitless. There are no language barriers. Popular American music has become the popular music of the entire world. What better form is there to promote understanding throughout the human race?

I have this fantasy about the future. I like to imagine somebody climbing into a spaceship and heading of to distant worlds. They pop their favorite music into the CD player, or DAT machine, or whatever device they have, and listen to records I helped make as they shoot off into distant space.

18

Putting it all in Perspective, 2010

Despite retirement sneaking up on me as the new millennium approached, there were some wonderful career surprises yet to come. I received a letter in 2000, notifying me of my induction into the Rock and Roll Hall of Fame – a real ego boost for me. Earl Palmer, Scotty Moore and I had been nominated and invited to the ceremonies at the Waldorf Astoria, in New York City. It had been over 40 years since I had played in the Waldorf, the last time being when I had the great fortune to work with the Count Basie band. As fate and bad timing would have it, a severe bronchial condition forced me to cancel out on the trip and my daughter Michelle attended on my behalf.

Somehow, though, that recognition brought to mind my uncle from Holyoke who watched me as a child as I practiced with my sticks pounding on a pillow, and who told me that I'd never amount to anything. All I knew was that, at 14, I was hooked on music, on the radio, and that I just wanted to be a drummer.

Thirty years later I was living in a Hollywood Hills mansion – the walls were covered with gold records and letters of commendation from all parts of the record business. The money was rolling in and I was on top of the world. I threw a lavish 50th wedding anniversary party for my parents, and when that bastard uncle walked in, I felt the satisfaction of payback time after his cruel and discouraging words during my teenage years. Not to be petty, but there is something sweet about proving your critics wrong.

And that mansion in the Hills was home to so many highs and lows in my life. The Stones came to the house, the Mamas and the Papas, and many other stars of the day. Brian Wilson loved that house so much he bought one very much like it in Bel Air. But my wife Lydia, after our daughter Michelle came along, found that she couldn't handle the show business lifestyle that came with the house, all the parties and celebrities hanging out there at all hours. Even with the many luxuries I afforded her, she decided to divorce me. Soon after, she took her own life, and Michelle and I were on our own.

I carry a lot of guilt, even today, for all that I put my little girl through in trying to find a replacement for her mother. I knew Michelle needed a mommy, and so I carelessly started marrying women as they entered my life. But it all became too much– too many women, too many divorces, too much heartache. Fortunately Michelle survived this period and went on to build a happy family of her own, with seven wonderful children!

But the lifestyle was one that I had to live, to do the things I was fortunate to have been able to accomplish. The Rock and Roll Hall of Fame induction was a result of being a part of Phil Spector's "Wall of Sound." That's the name people pinned on us, though we referred more to ourselves as The Wrecking Crew. But it was Phil who was one of the first producers to like my drumming, and he put me on the map with all of those hits he cooked up in the 50's and 60's. The world opened up for us core musicians, with producers coming to Hollywood from all over the world to hire the famed Wrecking Crew, and spread the success into their records.

It's funny how things come around again. Just when I thought that my world had crashed and burned, and all of the good times were behind me, the phones started ringing again due to old performances that had found their way back into circulation. Elvis Presley's *A Little Less Conversation*, for example – a song we originally recorded in 1968 – came back with a vengeance in the early 2000s. It showed up in many film and tv soundtracks, and, in 2007, it was chosen the official theme song of the 2007 NBA All-Star Game. It became a Number One hit all over the world, once again. I was doing interviews for a whole new generation of news media, now tuning in to Elvis on Satellite radio. Many of our old tracks were reemerging for a new audience, thanks to the new radio technology. Because of all this, I was once again being courted by the media to do interviews and talk about "back in the day..."

Unfortunately, at the same time the record industry was falling into chaos. The business had changed almost overnight, and the major labels were either folding, or just not signing new artists. The once mighty labels were mostly down to skeleton crews, most of the big moguls now gone, and the new people were mainly releasing re-packaged golden oldies.

I was happy to be semi-retired while this was all happening, though I was starting to get antsy in the relatively small place I had found in the town of Friendly Valley, California. After my life in big houses, this place was feeling more and more restrictive and the walls were closing in on me. I had fond memories of Palm Springs, from many years of traveling with Nancy Sinatra and occasionally dropping in on Frank at his great home in Rancho Mirage. I loved the clean air there and the feeling of lots of room and wide streets. But Palm Springs was for millionaires and so I decided to look for a place in the desert, not far away from Palm Springs, and a manageable distance from L.A.

A good friend had a daughter who turned me on to a realtor who took me and Michelle around the area until we found a perfect place in Palm Desert – red tile roof, pool, four bedrooms, and very quiet. Just what I was looking for, and my grandchildren helped me move in. I was excited to start this next phase of my life.

Being able to get to L.A. without much trouble came in handy, as there were increasing opportunities to stay plugged into the Hollywood scene, with the new attention that the Wrecking Crew had been receiving. Not the least of those opportunities came due to the tremendous documentary film that Denny Tedesco had been putting together for the past thirteen years.

Denny was the son of the late great Wrecking Crew guitarist Tommy Tedesco. Not only had Tommy and I played on hundreds of hit records and soundtracks together, but we were like family and had a deep love and respect for each other. Sadly Tommy was dying of cancer as Denny was finishing the documentary, and Denny worked feverishly to get as much of Tommy on film as possible in his final days. Tommy died before he was able to see the final release, but I'm sure he would have been so proud of Denny for the brilliant piece of work, and fitting testimony, he created.

This wonderful film has won many awards in film festivals and special screenings, and I am grateful to Denny for including me and Don Randi in many of those screenings, where we would answer questions, sometimes jam, and recount war stories of the good old days to enthusiastic audiences all over the country. Not only a wonderful retelling of the Wrecking Crew phenomenon, Denny's film is an inspiring perspective on the music of the 50's, 60's, 70's and 80's.

And Denny's work gave me renewed energy. Feeling now like

I was back into circulation, I greatly anticipated making the drive up Highway 5 to record with my dear old friend David "Dawg" Grisman. David, a supreme multi-instrumentalist who had defined his own blue-grass-influenced genre that everyone referred to as Dawg music, had invited me up to his new studio in Petaluma. It was February 1, 2003 when I hopped into my Eldorado and started the trek to what I knew would be a great week of fantastic music, no pressure, fun people and great restaurants. And I was ready for all of it.

Reaching his new studio I was greeted by his beautiful fiancée Tracy, who happened to also be a fine guitarist and graphic artist. The three of us instantly fell into a day of fun, trading jokes and scoping out the session we were going to start the next morning. Feeling charged up and happy for what was to come, I checked into my motel and slept like a baby.

The next morning I got up early and headed for the studio. My old friends at Zone Music had a beautiful set of Taye drums waiting for me in the corner. I added my own cymbals, the classic Zildjians that I'd used for nearly every style of music throughout my entire career. I was set up and ready to kick it hard. We ran down the first song a few times, then took a short break. As I was making a few notes on the drum part, my cell phone rang.

And that was the moment all Hell broke loose. It was my daughter, Michelle, on the other end. She was crying. I thought maybe something was wrong with one of her kids. Sobbing, she said, "Something happened at The Castle. The police are here and won't let me into my office."

Michelle, at that time, was Phil Spector's personal secretary and Girl Friday. Growing up in the business, she had been an avid music fan and adored Phil Spector, knowing that he was the master producer who had helped me immeasurably on the road to success, and we considered him a good friend. The Castle, where Phil ruled his empire and entertained the wealthy and powerful, had been built in the 1920's in Alhambra by an oil baron, and was on the list of "must see" landmark homes of California.

After Michelle calmed down enough to talk, she told me that the police had surrounded the house and no one was being let in or let out. Phil had been taken to jail. Helicopters were circling the mansion, and the press and paparazzi were swarming all over the scene, and Michelle could barely move from her car. "Daddy, the police said that someone was dead in the house and Phil is in jail and I don't know what to do!"

I told her to call Bob Shapiro, a friend of Phil's who had been part of the O.J. Simpson defense team, who I said would take care of everything. Michelle called Bob, who said that indeed he would take care of everything, but would need one and a half million dollars as a retainer. Michelle told him that she could only write a check for a million, and he agreed to take on the situation. Bob did what he promised, got Phil out of jail, making the Alhambra police look like they had beaten Phil to a pulp in the process.

With Michelle calmed down a bit, I returned to the Dawg sessions and finished my work. No sooner than getting back to my sweet little home in the desert I was bombarded with calls from journalists all over the world. Music magazine, newspaper, tv and entertainment reporters had gotten wind that I was known as Phil Spector's drummer, and they all wanted statements from me. I had no comment. I'd been out of town when this all happened, I told them.

I began speaking with Michelle every day, hearing all the lurid details and speculation, but somehow felt that Phil was very lucky and that he would beat this. Not more than a week after this new media circus had begun I received a call from the LA Weekly, a pretty powerful local news and entertainment paper. Of course I figured they wanted an interview about Phil as well, but I was wrong. They were actually calling to tell me that I had been chosen for a Lifetime Achievement Award as a person who helped create music that changed the world. Needless to say, I was flattered.

The presentation was at the Henry Fonda Theater, in Hollywood, and I had a large table reserved for friends and family. The night was very festive with speeches and bands playing, all for little ol' me. And then, surprise, surprise, Phil Spector walked in with a beautiful woman in tow, came over to my table, pulled my head back and planted a big kiss on my lips. He introduced his date and then said, "Hal, I've got to talk to you."

We moved over to a quiet spot and he said, "I want you to know that gal was a wannabe singer. I picked her up at the House of Blues and she asked if she could see The Castle. She was just getting off work as a hostess, so she grabbed a bottle of Tequila and we got into the limo. The bottle was half gone by the time we got to my place, 45 minutes away. She was pretty drunk, so I told the limo driver to take her home, but she insisted she wanted to see inside the place. I said OK and we went in, but she could barely walk, so again I told the driver to take her home and I went upstairs.

"When I came back down to have a snack a little later this

drunken woman was sprawled out on a chair in the foyer. Again, I told her that she'd have to leave and she started grabbing at me, giving me her showbiz spiel, "I want you to produce me! I'm a great singer!" She was loud and getting angry and then all of a sudden she pulled a pistol on me – where she got it, I have no idea. I said to put it away and instead she started to suck on the barrel of the gun, as if she was giving oral sex, murmuring, "I wanna do this to you, I'm gonna stay with you tonight, wouldn't you like that?"

"All of a sudden the gun went off. It was deafening. I hollered to the limo driver to call 911. He was in the car, right outside of the rear entrance."

Now I had no reason to not believe Phil. He'd never lied to me before, that I knew of anyway. He was at my special party, surprisingly happy and chipper, and I just figured that the poor guy had been through a very traumatic experience with a drunken fan. I really felt for him. He left shortly after that with his date, saying that he would return later, but never did, and that was the last time I ever spoke with him.

Later, when the LA detective unit questioned me I told them they were talking to the wrong person. I was just his drummer, never saw him with a gun, and never was part of his social circle. But I would never have lied to protect him anyway – it just wasn't my style.

As the weeks went on, I found my eyes glued to the then court TV channel. I watched intensely and listened to all the witnesses, especially the limo driver, and then realized that everything Phil had told me that night at the Henry Fonda Theater was as if he was a Times Square con artist, just working me. Go figure!

Though maybe not on the scale of Phil's saga, just about everyone, all over the world, has problems to deal with. Fortunately my many family problems now seemed to be behind me. My daughter was happily married, my bills were paid, and I was now happy living in my desert home. Nice things were starting to happen again, and my former life was paying dividends over and over.

One day, not long after the LA Weekly festivities, the phone rang and a gentleman introduced himself as Joseph Chambers, the owner/curator of the new Nashville Musicians' Hall of Fame and Museum. He was building a tribute to the unsung heroes of the recording industry, and wanted to meet while he was in Anaheim for the NAMM show and talk about his plans for the Hall of Fame.

These plans centered around choosing the studio recording groups from the major recording centers around the country and showcasing their contributions to our musical culture. He had picked the Wrecking Crew from Los Angeles, the "A" Team from Nashville, the Funk Brothers from Detroit, the Memphis Gang, the Blue Moon boys (Scotty Moore, Bill Black and DJ Fontana) and quite a few other behind-the-scenes legends. His plans included a major television special to kick off the Hall of Fame, and an annual awards show to add a few more inductees each year.

He wanted to start with the nucleus of each group, knowing that there were gray areas, people who played minor roles in each group, who might have to remain on the sidelines. He asked me to get in touch with the core of the Wrecking Crew. So I started making calls: Glen Campbell, Leon Russell, Lyle Ritz, Jimmy Bond, Don Randi, Joe Osborn, James Burton, Larry Knechtel, Billy Strange, Ray Pohlman, Earl Palmer, Julius Wechter, Jim Horn, Plas Johnson, Mike Deasy and Al DeLory – what I considered the "starter group" of the Wrecking Crew.

The problem was, no sooner did I start making these calls than the word spread like a California wildfire. I started getting calls from just about everyone I had ever worked with in a studio. They were crawling out of the woodwork, saying things like, "Hey, man, I thought that I was part of the Wrecking Crew!"

There turned out to be another 30 or 35 great musicians that I had cut hit records with at one point or another who felt like they were being overlooked. It took a lot of explaining to convince them that this first induction would just be for the original musicians, and that eventually they would all be added.

Meanwhile, Mr. Chambers was having many of my personal photos blown up for the display wall of our part of the exhibit. And, true to his word, it all happened just like he said. He flew us all in for a spectacular TV broadcast from the Schermer Symphony Hall in Nashville. He put us up in beautiful hotels for our rehearsal days and the show came off perfectly.

For the Wrecking Crew's portion of the show, we backed Vince Gill, Amy Grant, Brenda Lee, Rodney Crowell and Roger McGuinn, who many of us had recorded *Mr. Tambourine Man* with when he was the leader of the Byrds. Everyone was in great spirits and the reunions were a blast, visiting with old friends from long ago recording dates. We accepted our awards and did countless interviews with the media. The whole event could not have come off better, and Nashville's Southern hospitality was in full swing for us.

With my memory banks filled to the brim I returned home

to the desert, my favorite relaxation spot. But soon after I got back another surprise phone call added one more interesting twist into my ultra-eventful life. It was from Joy… who asked me if I remembered her.

Fifty years earlier, when I was traveling with the teen idol Tommy Sands, I was married to a wonderful lady named Joy. Joy eventually became Miss Nevada, but we had to get a quickie divorce in order to avoid a scandal, since she was not really a "Miss" at that time. If I'd had it to do over, I would have done everything I could to have stayed married to her. But I was on the road most of the time, respectful of this career opportunity for her, and with months apart from her, we just sort of drifted away from each other. She later got remarried, as did I, and that seemed to be the end of it.

Flash forward 50 years and here she is again, on the other end of my phone. Talk about second chances! We've spoken every day now for almost a year – a couple of senior citizens rediscovering each other, a truly wonderful experience and one that I look forward to every day.

Who knows what the future holds? When I started out in this life I certainly couldn't have imagined the path I would walk to get to my eightieth year. I chose the drums early in life, probably to get some attention. Little did I know that I would become one of the luckiest musicians to ever become involved in the music business. My ego has been way more than gratified.

At the same time, I feel like the guy who fell into the vat of chocolate – drowning from so many personal disasters, but what a sweet struggle it's been!

Hal Blaine Scholarship

The Hal Blaine Endowed Scholarship recognizes talented drummers and percussionists in the Performance Major at Berklee College of Music who demonstrate financial need.

Eligible Students:

Outstanding continuing student(s) with a demonstrated financial need who are enrolled at Berklee College of Music beginning in the fall of 2013 or, in the case that this endowed scholarship is established (fully paid) earlier than 2013, in the fall immediately following the date of establishment.

Checks should be paid to the order of: Berklee College of Music. The MEMO field of the check MUST say: Hal Blaine Scholarship Fund

Mail all donations to:

Berklee College of Music

attn: Peter Gordon

15303 Ventura Blvd, Suite 900

Sherman Oaks, CA 91403

For more information on the scholarship, please contact Peter Gordon directly: (818) 380-3041 or pgordon@berklee.edu

INDEX

Also from Rebeats

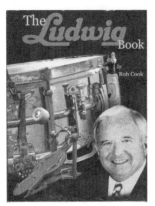

The Ludwig Book, by Rob Cook
Complete business history and dating guide for all catalogued snare drums, outfits, and production clues such as badges, colors, etc. Includes Ludwig & Ludwig, WFL, Leedy & Ludwig, Ludwig Industries, and today's Ludwig. Includes CDROM with today's Ludwig catalog, 1:1 scans of 1980s endorser posters, and rare audio recordings of WFL Jr. and WFL Sr.

The Making of A Drum Company:
The Autobiography of William F. Ludwig II
with Rob Cook
His whole story in his own words, from childhood recollections through teen years as a rudimental drum champion, wartime service, and the glory years of the Ludwig Drum Company.

Franks For The Memories
by Maurie Lishon, with Rob Cook
A history of the Legendary Franks Drum Shop of Chicago and the story of Maurie and Jan Lishon. Chapters on the Dixie Music House, Roy Knapp, Krupa, and more!!

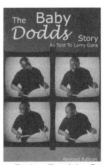

Gene Krupa, His Life & Times
by Bruce Crowther
Biography of Gene Krupa

The Baby Dodds Story;
As Told To Larry Gara
The autobiography of the famous New Orleans drummer that has inspired drummers from Gene Krupa to Steve Smith.

Also from Rebeats

The Rogers Book, Second Edition
by Rob Cook
A complete business history of the
Rogers drum company, and Rogers
drum dating guide.

The Slingerland Book, Second Edition
by Rob Cook
A complete business history of the
Slingerland drum company, and Slingerland
drum dating guide.

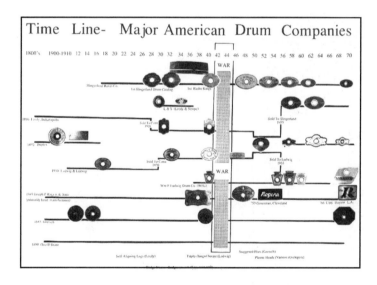

DRUM BADGE TIMELINE POSTER
18"x24" full color poster showing 85 drum
badges and their relative spots in drum history

A message from the producer of the documentary film
"The Wrecking Crew"

Growing up in the 60s, I was too young to go to the recording studios with my father, guitar player Tommy Tedesco, but I always knew the names of the other players.   There was one person who was very special in my father's life, his best friend Hal Blaine. They both grew up with very humble beginnings, one Jewish and one Italian. But their love of music brought them together to Hollywood where fairy tales really can come true.

Part of the job as a leader on a session was to create an atmosphere of creativity, and Hal was known to bring out the best in everyone. My father used to say that it didn't matter if the job was for Sinatra or for the 'kid' next door, Hal Blaine gave 110% and was only interested in making it a hit record.

Tommy & Hal were not only great musicians but great men. They were brothers in and out of the studios.   Both had an extreme sense of humor that helped to lighten up the seriousness of their day jobs and both looked out for their friends. When one was down the other tried to lift his spirits.

When I started *The Wrecking Crew* Documentary my father was terminally ill with cancer. He was my mentor and best friend as well as my father. A year after he passed away I went back to filming the story, and although it took another 10 years to finally finish the film, there was no way I could have done it without Hal.   When I had doubt or fear I turned to Hal for encouragement, which was always there 110%, for which I will be forever grateful.   Our relationship has developed over the years to where Hal is now my mentor, my best friend and a father figure to me.

Hal has graced millions of people around the world with his music, but I am so fortunate to be graced with his love.

Denny Tedesco
November, 2009